HIDDEN GLASGOW

LET GLASGOW FLOURISH

HIDDEN GLASGOW

CAROL FOREMAN

First published in Great Britain in 2001
by John Donald, an imprint of
Birlinn Ltd
West Newington House
10 Newington Road
Edinburgh
EH9 1QS

www.birlinn.co.uk

ISBN 0 85976 545 8

British Library Cataloguing-in-Publication Data
A catalogue record for this book is available on request from the British Library

Design by Mark Blackadder

Printed and bound by The Cromwell Press, Trowbridge, Wiltshire

CONTENTS

INTRODUCTION

Defining what is hidden in a city is not easy. What is commonplace to some locals is not to others and what is commonplace to locals is surprising to visitors.

Aspects of 'Hidden' Glasgow can vary from buildings that are not open to the public to some that are hidden by others or are enveloped by additions, like the Gallery of Modern Art, which has an 18th-century mansion in its midst.

Some things might be hidden merely by virtue of being off the beaten track, while the plain façades of some buildings, like 22 Park Circus, hide the sumptuousness of their interiors. Then again, sometimes the impressive appearance of the outside of a building hides a neglected grandeur, as in Laurieston House in Carlton Place.

Some treasures, like the Lady Well, are hidden because they alone have survived amid a landscape radically changed over the decades or even centuries.

Some works of art can be found only by looking down or by looking up, like the golden merchant ship on top of the dome of the Merchants' House, which it takes a very keen eye to spot. Other gems have simply been forgotten about, such as the abandoned Britannia Music Hall in Argyle Street and the time-warp schoolroom discovered in the attic of the Trades House.

Often things are hidden because we are far too busy rushing past to notice them or because we do not expect them to be there, like the delightful mini park in Garnethill, created out of a rat-ridden crater. Sometimes we don't realise that some buildings are not what they seem, such as the Ramshorn Church, which is now a theatre.

The secrets of some buildings lie beneath them, like Central Station and the Mitchell Library. Some even lie beneath the River Clyde, like the old Harbour Tunnel.

Some buildings are taken for granted by locals, who have never been inside them, like the magnificent City Chambers. Other buildings have attractions that are not generally open to the public, such as the Strathclyde Police Museum in Pitt Street.

It's not only buildings and objects that can be hidden: events have often been hidden because they do not reflect well on the city, like the Lock Hospital for 'dangerous women', which Glasgow pretended didn't exist.

All these hidden aspects of Glasgow and many more, like a Rennie Mackintosh building hidden down a lane and what it's like inside the Tolbooth Steeple, will be unlocked in *Hidden Glasgow,* which I hope you will enjoy.

CAROL FOREMAN

CHAPTER I

THE CITY CHAMBERS

George Square

It may seem strange to start a book called *Hidden Glasgow* with an article about the City Chambers, the city's largest public building. However, it's not as strange as you might think because, although the outside of the building is known to all and sundry, many Glaswegians have never set foot inside it, which means its magnificent interior is hidden from them.

The City Chambers shows, more clearly than any other building in the city, the opulence of Glasgow in its Victorian heyday. Its lavishness leaves no doubt as to the city's wealth and importance as the second city of the British Empire. The building is now the headquarters of Glasgow City Council, and the fifth to be used for civic purposes.

The foundation stone was laid on 6 October 1883, an unforgettable day, with 600,000 spectators watching as a trades procession and a civic-masonic procession converged on George Square. Four years later, the

Drawing of the 'New Municipal Buildings' showing Lord Provost Ure and architect William Young

building's topmost stone, the apex of the central tower, was laid and, on 22 August 1888, Queen Victoria performed the inauguration ceremony. The first council meeting took place on 10 October 1889. A ten-day public viewing in 1889 attracted 400,000 people.

The design of the new City Chambers was the result of two competitions that had drawn hundreds of submissions. Paisley-born, but London-based, William Young was the winner, a choice much criticised, with reason, by local architects.

As the building occupies the whole of the east side of George Square, it is memorable for its huge physical presence and, despite its outward appearance, is built of bricks, over ten million of them, faced with stone.

Young described the architecture of the building as 'a free and dignified treatment of the Italian Renaissance'. The general height of the walls is 75 feet above street level, with the corners, crowned with octagonal cupolas, reaching up one storey higher than the rest of the building. Undoubtedly, however, the finest feature is the elevation facing George Square, which has a 216-foot central tower and a pediment showing an enthroned Queen Victoria, supported by figures representing Scotland, Ireland, England and Wales, receiving the homage and congratulations of her subjects from all parts of the world. Three figures surmount the apex – the central one symbolises Truth, holding aloft the Light of Liberty, whose bright rays are supposed to spread over the city; the other two figures represent Riches and Honour.

Loggia with its allegedly 1.5 million different pieces of mosaic

The main entrance is inspired by the historical Arch of Constantine in Rome, the keystone of the centre arch bearing the city of Glasgow's arms with the motto 'Let Glasgow Flourish'. As the supporting figures represent Religion, Virtue and Knowledge, when taken as a whole, they embody the idea of the older form of the motto: 'Let Glasgow Flourish by the Preaching of the Word'.

Magnificent though the exterior of the City Chambers is, the true expression of Victorian opulence comes within. The entrance hall, or Loggia, as Young called it, is overwhelmingly sumptuous, reminiscent of the most luxurious hotel. In fact, tourists trailing their suitcases behind them have approached the reception desk and asked if they were in Central Hotel.

For beauty of proportion, harmonious blending of stone, granite, marble and mosaic, the Loggia is unique, at least in this country. Architecturally, it resembles the plan of a Roman church of the Renaissance period, the centre and side arches corresponding to the nave and aisles, and the extending intercepting arch to the transept. Coupled columns of Scottish red granite, supported on bases of grey Aberdeen granite and topped by Ionic capitals of Tuscan dark green marble, carry the arches. Young spent a lot of time in Italy, which is where his ideas came from.

The brilliant glazed ceramic Venetian mosaic covering the vaulted ceiling and domes enhances the beautiful effect of the Loggia. Pompeian in character, the design is said to contain just over 1.5 million different pieces of mosaic. (They are half-inch cubes, every one inserted by hand, and how it's known there are just over 1.5 million is curious. Did someone count them?) As the colour goes right through the mosaic, the decoration is practically imperishable. Just in case anyone might have the idea that foreign craftsmen were responsible for the fine work, it was all done by Glasgow men employed by Glasgow firms. There's more mosaic on the floor, with the city's coat of arms in its original form inlaid just inside the entrance.

Hanging from the ceiling are the original lamps of 1888, which are of wrought iron filled with Venetian glass. When the building was opened, it had a steam-driven generator in the basement that powered enough electricity to light up the Loggia, the Lord Provost's office, the Council Chamber and the Banqueting Hall. Everywhere else had to make do with gas. At the time the decision to have electric lighting was innovative.

From the Loggia, four doorways (now unused) give access to the staircases, the two facing the entrance having pedimented overdoors supported by Greek caryatids (female figures) representing Wisdom, Purity, Strength and Honour. The other two have richly carved panels with four life-sized figures in the spandrels interpreting the inscription originally carved on the old Glasgow Tolbooth, the City Chambers of the day. The inscription read:

'To this house vice is hateful,
By this house peace is beloved.
By this house upright men are honoured
And evil doers are punished.'

The staircases are to the left and right of the Loggia, the left one being the magnificent Banqueting Staircase of solid-veined Carrara marble, the largest three-storey marble staircase in Europe, the closest to it being in Vatican City. (It has served as a television location for Vatican City.) To the right is the Council Chamber Staircase, which, being made of freestone, is known as the Black Staircase. The balusters of both stairs are alabaster.

If the Loggia is stunning, the Council Chamber Staircase, with its breathtaking display of richly variegated marbles harmoniously blended with

Council Chamber Staircase with 'Lucky Lion of the Chambers' at the foot of the first flight

alabaster, is even more so. (There are three different varieties of marble in the building, all Italian.) The marble lion guarding the staircase on the first floor is named the 'Lucky Lion of the Chambers'. He's supposed to bring good luck to those who pat him on the head when passing. As to whether he does, as far as is known, no one working in the building has won the lottery.

There are graffiti on the half-landing leading to the second floor and there are two stories as to how they got there. One is that, during the First World War, when the building was under martial law and guarded 24 hours a day, the half-landing was a sentry post and, to while away the hours, some sentries carved their initials and the date in the marble with their bayonets. The other version is that it was the handiwork of journalists who used to group on the half-landing while waiting to be addressed by the Lord Provost.

On the second floor, where the Banqueting Staircase and the Council Chamber Staircase connect, there's a spellbinding vista of marble halls, arches and vaulted, richly plastered ceilings. The second floor houses the Council Chamber, reception salons, Banqueting Hall, Lord Provost's Suite and the 200-foot-long Councillors' Corridor, where the committee rooms and the Library are situated. With its domed roof decorated in yellow, blue, brown and white faïence (a form of glazed and decorated pottery first made at Faenza in Italy), the Corridor looks like something out of *The Arabian Nights*.

The 'Arabian Nights' Councillors' Corridor

The Council Chamber is where the Council meets formally. Facing George Square, it's an impressive room, with Spanish mahogany panelling and a massive mahogany fireplace at each end with the city's coat of arms in the centre. At the north end, the fireplace has been adapted into a small gallery for the press. Above the panelling, the greenish-gold border is not wallpaper, but leather-embossed Tynecastle tapestry. The magnificent, richly coloured gilded ceiling has a central dome, filled, like the stained-glass windows, with greenish-patterned glass. The three massive electroliers are the original 1888 ones. Unfortunately, the shades look more like British Home Stores 1988.

The horseshoe seating, fitted in 1912 when the city was extended, faces the platform, where the Lord Provost, Deputy Lord Provost and Chief Executive sit behind the mace, which has to be in place before a full Council meeting can start. Each councillor has a designated seat. Behind the councillors is an area called the 'Bed Recess' – a reference to a feature of old Glasgow tenements. Council officials sit there, along with the Lord Dean of Guild, representing the Merchants' House, and the Deacon Convener of the Trades House, the city's second and third citizens. Immediately above the 'Bed Recess' is a public gallery.

The Lord Provost's chair was a gift from Queen Victoria when the

Council Chamber

inauguration took place. She also presented a carnation to each councillor, which began a tradition. Before the start of each full meeting of the Council, a carnation is placed in the little hole beside each councillor's microphone. (The Parks Department supplies the flowers.)

Of the three reception rooms lying between the Council Chamber and the Banqueting Hall, the first, the Satinwood Salon, is designated the 'municipal drawing room'. Its entire woodwork – doors, windows and panelling – is a light-coloured Australian satinwood.

In the room are two paintings from the city's art collection, both by E. A. Hornell, one of the famous 'Glasgow Boys' school of painters. The larger, *Spring Roundelay* (1910), shows seven children having fun. Scrutiny of the painting reveals that all the children have the same face. Apparently, Hornell always used his niece's face as a model and just changed the expression to make it look different. The smaller painting, *Blue Flax*, was stolen from the City Chambers in the 1990s. Two men dressed in overalls walked in, took it off the wall and then walked out of the back door with it. As the painting was too well known in the art world for the thieves to sell, however, a few days later, after an anonymous phone call to the Council, it turned up in a telephone box in the East End of the city.

Connecting with the Satinwood Salon is the Octagonal Room,

The magnificent barrel-vaulted Banqueting Hall decorated with murals depicting scenes from Glasgow's history

panelled in amberwood, which is darker than satinwood. The darker tone of the amberwood prepares the eye for the rich deep colour of the adjoining Mahogany Salon, the last of the suite of reception rooms.

The Mahogany Salon leads to the Banqueting Hall, which, despite fierce competition from the Loggia, the Council Chamber and its Carrara staircase, is the City Chambers' *pièce de résistance*.

The vast double-height barrel-vaulted Banqueting Hall clearly shows the influence of the French buildings visited by the Council's advisory committee. Although early Renaissance in style, much of the wall decoration is in the form of huge murals painted by the 'Glasgow Boys', then the most modern work the city could offer. Architect William Leiper supervised the work depicting some of Glasgow's history.

The lunette over the platform has George Henry's mural representing King William the Lion granting the charter for the institution of the Glasgow Fair. On the south wall, nearest the stage, is Alexander Roche's *Legendary Glasgow*, portraying St Mungo taking a ring from the mouth of a salmon, one of the legendary stories surrounding the city's coat of arms. Edward Walton's *Glasgow Fair at the End of the 15th Century* is in the centre, and Sir John Lavery's *Modern Glasgow*, representing local industry, is to its right. In Roche's and Walton's murals, the figures were friends of the artists. George Henry, however, went further, his figures being well-known public figures in the West of Scotland, such as Samuel Chisholm, who became Lord Provost of Glasgow in 1899. Apart from the murals, the walls are panelled in Spanish mahogany.

Above the doors, four panels represent Scotland's principal rivers – the Tay, the Forth, the Clyde and the Tweed. Above these, and in the spaces between the windows, is Alexander Walker's interpretation of various virtues – Modesty, Faith, Hope, Charity, Mercy, etc. The floor-to-ceiling double-glazed windows are in grey-leaded Venetian glass, the centre one commemorating Queen Victoria's Diamond Jubilee. Incidentally, the Hall's four pedimented mahogany doors are not all they seem. To add symmetry to the back wall, the first and third are false.

The Banqueting Hall's coffered barrel-vaulted ceiling can hold its own against any that Venice can offer. Its magnificent plasterwork has 117 panels decorated in turquoise and masses of gold shading to a coppery colour. In fact, the first impression is of a sea of gold or, more correctly, a sky of gold, until a closer look reveals the turquoise.

A tour of the City Chambers ends in the oval Louis XVI-style gallery, where the portraits of former Lord Provosts are on view. Among them is that of Lord Provost Ure, who laid the foundation stone in 1883. Another portrait is of William Collins (Provost, 1877), famous for allowing only iced water to be served at civic functions. There is a drinking fountain in Glasgow Green commemorating his work for the temperance cause. The barrel-vaulted ceiling, has a riot of ornamental plasterwork. The colour scheme is Wedgwood-blue, white and gold and in the centre is the fabulous glass dome with kaleidoscopic tints, which is visible from the other floors. A lean over the wrought-iron balustrade reveals tier upon tier of marble and alabaster pillars and arches reaching all the way down to the Loggia.

The free, twice-daily tours of the City Chambers on weekdays are not to be missed. Never again will there be a palace like the Chambers built in Glasgow.

Oval Portrait Gallery

CHAPTER 2

NEXT IN IMPORTANCE

Clyde Port Building, Robertson Street

Just as few Glaswegians have seen the interior of the City Chambers, few have seen the sumptuous interior of the building next in importance to it – the Clyde Port building, at the south-east corner of Robertson Street. When it was built, the Clyde Navigation Trust rivalled what was then Glasgow Corporation in power and influence, and, as befitted its status, its headquarters were little short of the City Chambers in architectural interest. The splendour of the building's interior was not for the benefit of the public but solely for the Trustees and their visitors.

Today, the building is owned by Clydeport PLC, whose origins go back to 1759, when a Clyde Trust was formed, under the direct control of the Corporation, to regulate trade and activity on the River Clyde. Then, the river was a comparatively small stream full of shoals and shifting sand banks, and navigable only by boats carrying a few tons. It was not until 1775 that vessels

Floodlit Clyde Port Building

drawing six feet of water were able to come up to the Broomielaw at high tide.

In 1966 the Clyde Navigation Trust, the Greenock Harbour Trust and the Clyde Lighthouses Trust merged to become the Clyde Port Authority, which, in 1992, became Clydeport PLC after a management and employee buyout. Today, the company owns approximately 450 square miles of land and water, from slightly upriver of its headquarters down to a line running through the isle of Arran.

One of the riverside's most famous landmarks is the crane at Finnieston, erected by the Trust in 1931 specifically for loading railway locomotives on to ships bound for the far corners of the Empire and beyond. (Glasgow was the largest builder of railway locomotives in the world outwith North America.) At 185 feet high, with a jib length of 258 feet and a lifting capacity of 250 tons, it was the largest crane in the world. Restored in 1995 as a symbol of the past importance of the River Clyde, the Finnieston Crane (officially the Stobcross Crane) is a Grade A-listed building, which means it cannot be demolished or altered in any way. In 1931, the crane cost £52,351 to build. Today, it costs more than that to paint it.

The Clyde Port building is also A-listed and constitutes only two stages of the four originally intended, which would have made the building almost as large as the City Chambers. Architect J. J. Burnet began phase one

Pillared and arched Trustees' Corridor

in 1882 and added phase two, at the corner of Robertson Street, in 1908. Impressive though the building is, it has an unbalanced and unfinished look. The five-bay pedimented unit, topped by a colossal statue of Poseidon and seahorses, was obviously intended as the centre of a huge building reaching up Robertson Street.

The sumptuous suite consisting of Trustees' Corridor, former Trust Board Room, Committee Rooms and Trust Hall is on the second floor. Instead of taking the lift up to it, it is better to use the massive grand staircase, as it is lit at the foot by a fabulous 15-foot-high metal newel-post-cum-lamp-standard, with Roman-prow cantilever brackets holding lightshades.

Even the Trustees' Corridor, which provides access to all the rooms, is magnificent, with French walnut and teak panelling, gilded domes supported on black and gold pillars with gold-leaf Corinthian capitals, mosaic flooring and stained-glass windows with the trades' badges – fleshers, coopers, bakers, dyers, skinners, etc.

The splendid Trust Hall, which replaced the original Board Room, is in the 1908 phase of the building. No one could fail to be impressed by the circular room, French Baroque in style and decorated in aquamarine, white and gold. It has a 30-feet-high domed ceiling and a floor with the centre sunk down two steps into a well shape. (The well was not part of the original layout. It dates from 1966, when the Trust became the Clyde Port Authority.)

Particularly stunning are the colourful windows by Stephen Adam, which represent shipbuilding, commerce and engineering. With the light flooding through them, the rich harmony of colour is startling. Unlike church stained-glass windows, which are usually in small sections surrounded by lead, these are in large sections and, although they are believed to be stained glass, they look as if they are painted, which is possible, as Stephen Adam's forte was to paint a scene and fire it on to the glass. Whatever method he used, the result is stunning.

Standing inside the huge bay of the window facing west along the Broomielaw gives an impression of being almost on top of the water. It's easy to imagine the old Trustees, dressed in frock coats, standing in the same spot, surveying what was then a bustling noisy harbour, with ships moored as many as five abreast. It was just 600–700 yards downriver from the window that ships left daily for Dublin and Belfast. The passengers' embarkation shed was where a casino now stands.

There is much in the Trust Hall to wonder at – walnut and ebony panelling, decorative plasterwork and white marble Ionic pillars dividing the room into eight bays, the most elaborate being the one where the chairman and members of the old Trust sat. The pillars on either side of this bay are topped by plaster female figures, the one on the right holding a globe, the one on the left a ship. Between the figures is an elaborate plaster arch framing a stained-glass window crowned by the original Clyde Navigation Trust crest.

The original Trust Board Room is astonishing, for the ceiling looks like the structure of an old wooden ship turned upside down. Sections between the ribs have been picked out in red and peacock-blue. The walls are three-quarters panelled with French walnut banded with ebonised wood, above which is a wallcovering embossed with nine-carat gold leaf.

There are three stained-glass windows representing Glasgow Corporation, the Merchants' House, the Trades' House, the Chamber of Commerce and the Clydeside burghs. The burgh's coats of arms appear

J.J. Burnet's superb Trust Hall showing bay where the chairman and members of the old Trust sat

because, in 1886–88 there were 25 Trustees who were selected from areas on either side of the Clyde. The centre window incorporates the Clyde navigational seal – a large sailing ship on top of a Glasgow coat of arms, below which is a large anchor. The Glasgow coat of arms appears over the huge sliding doors at each end of the room, overhung so that they push open with two fingers. The mechanism works from Viking-style brass straps across the top.

Above the fireplace, rolled up one behind the other, are two maps (about 20 feet in width) printed on old sailcloth. One is of the Clyde in its infancy, the other of the world. The maps should pull down but, as the last time it was attempted, they began to tear, the Trust thought it best not to try again.

What a marvellous job Burnet did for the Clyde Trust, giving the room a nautical feel with his splendid boat-shaped ceiling and Viking-style door hangings.

Those lucky enough to visit the building leave it marvelling at its richness and beauty, and at the part the Trust played in developing the River Clyde from a shallow stream full of shoals and shifting sand banks into a legend in maritime history.

Original Board Room showing Viking-style door hangings with Glasgow's coat of arms above them. The magnificent light fittings are suspended on 15-foot poles

CHAPTER 3

A MYTH DISPELLED

Beneath Central Station

The following will dispel, once and for all, the myth that hidden beneath Central Station is a village of cobbled streets, houses and shops. For years there have been folk tales that the station was built on top of the village of Grahamston, whose main street was Alston Street. It was not. The village was demolished, and what lies beneath the concourse and platforms of Central Station is a profusion of passages, open spaces, tunnels and arches reaching into the bowels of the building.

Underground, the station is far larger than the areas open to the public. Along corridors and across open spaces, it goes down and down until the clanking and thumping of the trains become so faint they can barely be heard. The heat is stifling.

Apart from the areas taken up by Red Star, the catering department for inter-city trains, the lost-property store, the boiler room and two model railway clubs, much of the vast underground space is unused. A remnant of the past is a huge caged warehouse, once used to store contraband taken from trains – drink, cigarettes, pornographic material, drugs, etc. All the fire exits from the shops in Union Street and Argyle Street that back on to the station lead into its warren of underground corridors.

Although throughout the underground sections of the station there are shadows of yesteryear, going through a red door into the arches is like walking into the past. The arches, which are almost like catacombs with blackened walls and a musty earthy smell, were used as workshops when the station was being built. They were once full of men toiling in intense heat, and there are reminders of the work that went on there – a series of knee-high brick walls used to support huge boilers to make it easier for the engineers to work on them; a large gas cylinder, called an econotimer, and pressure gauges on the wall for oil tanks. Curiously, there's even a Plimsoll line on a wall. What it was used for is anyone's guess, but it could have been that water from some underground stream poured into the arches at one time and, if it got above a certain level, it was time to evacuate them. That explanation is quite feasible, as at one time a stream ran down the area that is now West Nile Street and Mitchell Street.

One arch was possibly used as a forge or for brick-making, as it has the remnants of a furnace set into the wall and a concrete platform on the floor. Another arch has a low narrow tunnel leading off from both sides. Where the tunnels originally went no one knows, as now they come to a dead end. It's thought, however, that they were once higher and that at some time the floors were filled in.

Although the arches are not used any more, empty cigarette packets, Coke cans, a half-full bottle of Irn Bru and newspapers lie among the rubble. Not the most pleasant place to have an unofficial break but certainly out of the way.

Fascinating though the arches are, it's a relief to leave them and get back to the concourse, as the stifling heat and musty smell become overpowering. Also, it's rather frightening knowing how far below ground the arches are.

From top to bottom, the station is shaped like an inverted pyramid, and it's possible from below ground to walk from platform ten to platform one in a fraction of the time it takes to get there across the concourse. It's the same from the Ladies' and Gent's Superloos – below ground they are just next to each other; above ground they are at opposite ends of the station. As a long distance across the concourse becomes a short distance underground, there is a good case for using some below-ground space to ease congestion between platforms above ground. Platforms seven, eight, nine and ten connect below ground.

Central Station opened on 1 August 1879. Built by the Caledonian Railway at a cost of £2 million, it had 80,000 square yards of rubble in its foundations. Twenty thousand tons of concrete, 10 million bricks and 14,000 tons of cast iron were used in its construction. 'A very handsome structure', reported one newspaper,

> 'with a frontage to Gordon Street and Hope Street of 536 ft rising to 112 ft above sea level. Three of the platforms [there were six initially] are 800 ft in length and stretch right across the bridge at Argyle Street. . . . To bear the enormous weight of the roof, the side walls have been made of great strength, each of the 17 massive girders being supported by pilasters of six feet of solid masonry.'

When the station opened, it had 134 daily services. By 1887 it had over 300. Between 1879 and 1887 Glasgow's population exploded, and Central, with a layout regarded as adequate to cope with the then-foreseeable increase in traffic, suddenly became too small. It was therefore decided to enlarge it.

Reconstruction began in 1901 and was completed in 1905. It was one of the most costly engineering projects undertaken by the Caledonian Railway. A massive new bridge was built across the River Clyde and the station was extended westwards towards Hope Street. Initially there were loud protests when the Argyle Street bridge became a tunnel. However, once it was lined with shops and people realised it provided free shelter from bad weather, it became a meeting place – the famous Hielanman's Umbrella, which underwent an award-winning refurbishment in 1999.

The Umbrella was in the news the day that the Stone of Destiny came back to Scotland. There was a report that a package had been planted somewhere in it. The bomb squad was called in, and the station had to close down and the trains stop, as any vibration could have set off a bomb. Fortunately, it turned out to be a hoax by a group trying to make a name for itself.

Platform space was increased to thirteen (the same number as today) and, in 1905, the Central's famous train indicator made its first appearance, as reported in the press: 'For the assistance of passengers and of occasionally forgetful members of staff, there is a train indicator, so placed that there is no part of the concourse from which it is not visible, and it is of such generous proportions that he who runs (to catch his train) may read without diminishing aught of his haste.' (Obviously Edwardian ladies did not run for trains.) The manual indicator has been replaced by a restaurant and shops, and the largest electronic train indicator in Europe now gives passengers information about departures, arrivals and delays.

Below the concourse, the 1905 revamp gave Central an enormous gent's lavatory with marble floors, heaters, copper towel rails and three sumptuous bathrooms. Tonsorial artists were in attendance.

By 1907, Central handled a daily average of 600 trains, or one every two minutes at the busiest parts of the day. The strictest organisation was required to prevent them from treading on each other's heels and, as a precaution, the 'dead end' of each platform had emergency hydraulic buffers installed that could stop a 400-ton train travelling at twelve miles an hour 'without shock'. When the station celebrated its centenary in 1979, 1,000 trains a day were logged.

While computers now record arrivals and departures, when Central opened, they were timed by a railwayman carrying the traditional 'reliable' railway timekeeper, a steel-cased pocket watch he carried in his waistcoat pocket.

Despite cosmetic changes, Central would still be recognisable to an early-20th-century commuter. Gone, however, is the 'Shop Parcels' department, which offered a service to lady shoppers from out of town. After buying what they wanted from the stores, the ladies didn't need to struggle through the streets with their purchases or hire a taxi – a station porter collected their packages and took them to the station to be picked up later.

Gone also are the famous concourse newspaper kiosks that stood in the middle of the station. One of these, occupied by John Menzies & Co., was smashed to smithereens in October 1904, when a train was being shunted into platform seven in preparation for its trip to London at 10.45 pm. The propulsive force given to the carriages was greater than the distance required, with the result that the guard's van crashed into and demolished the buffer stops and, mounting the platform with tremendous force, crashed into the bookstall, completely smashing it. Fortunately, there were only three employees in the stall and one customer in front of it, all of whom miraculously escaped with minor injuries. Apart from the carriage that crashed into the stall, the London train was undamaged and left at its scheduled time.

A massive refurbishment of the Grade A-listed building began in 1997 and was completed in 2000, a year ahead of schedule and 15 per cent under budget. The work included replacing the magnificent glass roof that

Photograph of Central Station in 1910, which shows that it has not changed much since then except that the newspaper kiosk no longer exists. (Courtesy of Bill Howard, printed from original Taxiphote slide)

stretches from Gordon Street to the River Clyde. The station is the largest public building under glass in the UK. The roof, which has 50,000 panes of glass, covers six acres – three times the size of Hampden Park.

While there have been downsides to the privatisation of the railway system, without it there would have been no refurbishment of the station and its crime rate would not have dropped by 30 per cent, thanks to the introduction of security cameras.

Most of us never think about what is involved in running a station, other than that the trains should arrive and depart on time. However, there is much more to it than that. In fact, the station manager and staff are responsible for everything except running the trains. Among those responsibilities are personnel, security, safety, catering, retail outlets, dealing with thousands of football fans travelling to Hampden for an international game and even organising a search for a missing child. While to write down the job description of the station manager of today would take up a few pages, at least he doesn't have to wear a top hat and sport a flower in his buttonhole as his Victorian counterpart did.

Someone must be doing something right at Central, Scotland's largest station, with 94,000 travellers using it every day, as it currently holds the UK titles of Station of the Year, Major Station of the Year, Most Passenger-Friendly Station and Scotland Zone Station of the Year.

Next time you are in the station, take a bit more time to appreciate it, but remember, there is no village hidden beneath it.

Central Station during the Second World War, showing one of the famous John Menzies newspaper kiosks

CHAPTER 4

ON TOP OF THE WORLD

Merchants' House, George Square

Being right in the heart of the city, the Merchants' House seems hardly the place to look for hidden treasures. It is, however, but to find one of them, a pair of binoculars is useful as it is perched on the top of the building's corner dome. It's a golden fully rigged ship atop a globe, a replica of that topping the 164-foot-high steeple of the original Merchants' House in the Briggait. The steeple, which still stands, was described as 'being of curious architecture with three battlements above one another and a curious clock of molten brass, the spire of which has a ship of copper in place of a weathercock'.

Apart from the golden ship, the other hidden treasures are to be found inside the building. They tell of the antiquity of the esteemed institution, and two of them are quaintly sculptured stones salvaged from the Briggait building. One shows a full-sailed galleon riding the waves, while the

Façade of Merchants' House

Old stones salvaged from the old Merchants' House in the Briggait. One shows a full-sailed galleon riding the waves while the other shows three bearded, voluminously cloaked old men leaning on long staves

other depicts three bearded, voluminously cloaked old men leaning on long staves. A peculiarity of the men, thought to be merchants and described in Denholm's *History of Glasgow* as 'the three old men in the habit of Pilgrims', is that they seem to be standing on their toes.

Another stone has the words GLASGOW and MERCAT, a bell, a ship and a large figure 4 cut into it. (The figure 4, used in various forms, was the symbol of Glasgow's merchants and features in the Merchants' House's crest.) There is some controversy about the origins of this stone. At first it was said to have come from the old Mercat Cross, but later, because of the markings, especially the figure 4, it was believed to have come from the region of Glasgow Cross and was actually from the Merchants' House in the Briggait.

Displayed in a glass case in the Directors' Room is a model of a tobacco ship of 1740, attributed to a Dutch apprentice working in a Clyde yard about 1810. The ship is a barque, readily identifiable by the mix of square and fore-and-aft sails. There is a similar model, almost certainly by the same apprentice, in Amsterdam.

Also in the Directors' Room is a marble neoclassical relief built above the mantelpiece, commemorating Archibald Ingram, Dean of Guild and Lord Provost in the mid 18th century. A kneeling Ingram is about to have a wreath placed on his head by the Genius of Glasgow, while three female figures, said to represent Commerce, Architecture and Civic Rule, stand behind him. The sculpture, presented to the Merchants' House in 1809 by a member of the Ingram family, was put aside and forgotten about until 1859, when it was unearthed and put on display. Curiously, almost simultaneously with the

Model of a tobacco ship of 1740 made by a Dutch apprentice working in a Clyde yard about 1810

sculpture's discovery, a descendant of Provost Ingram in London enquired as to what had become of it.

On the first landing of the George Square staircase there is a larger-than-life statue of Kirkman Finlay attired as an ancient Roman. It is the work of James Gibson (a Welsh sculptor and a favourite with Queen Victoria), and many people visit the Merchants' House just to see it. Apparently, so that he could study anatomy, Gibson used to go out with body-snatchers but had to stop because of the terrible nightmares he suffered.

Kirkman Finlay (1773–1842) was one of Glasgow's greatest merchants, if not *the* greatest. He was elected a Member of Parliament in 1812 when he was also Provost of Glasgow. When he died, his obituary in *The Glasgow Herald* said he was the 'Beau-ideal of a Glasgow Merchant'. It also made the point about the incredible growth of trade that had taken place with the Orient and how a trip to the Broomielaw would reveal ships bound for Calcutta, Bombay, Singapore, Manila and ports all over the east. His mercantile genius gave Glasgow an astonishing position in the Eastern and China trade. Although Kirkman is said to haunt the Merchants' House, the consensus is that he is s friendly spirit, not a malevolent one.

The Merchants' House, at the north-west corner of George Square, was designed in 1877 by John Burnet, with his son John James Burnet adding two storeys in 1909. Reaching round to West George Street, it's an impressive building, with three richly decorated oriel windows supported by sculptures by James Young of caryatids (female figures) and atlantes (male figures). Unfortunately, the addition of the two upper storeys spoiled the symmetry of the west side of George Square.

Sculpture commemorating Archibald Ingram, Lord Provost of Glasgow in the mid 18th century

CHAPTER 5

GLASGOW'S SECRET SHAME

Lock Hospital. Rottenrow

Glasgow's secret shame is the Lock Hospital for 'dangerous women' with sexually transmitted diseases, the hospital the city pretended didn't exist.

The Lock Hospital is one of Glasgow's best-kept secrets. It was buried deep in the city's history and all knowledge of it denied. That is, until librarian Anna Forrest, who refused to believe it never existed, brought the dark secrets of its history to light. She pored over Glasgow's burgh records, the city planning office notes and records of the city's hospitals for five years before concluding her account of the 'non-existent' place.

Anna's goal was to give a voice to those so-called dangerous women who were made scapegoats for the spread of venereal diseases. Polite society did not want to know when the proposal to open a VD medical centre for women was considered in 1805, a feeling reflected in the lack of documentation about the Lock Hospital.

The Glasgow Lock Hospital borrowed its name from the first established Lock Hospital in London, founded in 1746 in Southwark, reputedly on the site of a former leper house. 'Lock' derives either from the Old English word *loke* (a leper house) or from the Old French *loque*, meaning rags, bandages or lints used to clean or scrape the sores of lepers before entering the leper house. Like lepers, those with VD were shunned.

Until the Lock opened in Glasgow, women had no sexual health care. In fact, throughout the 18th century it was thought that finding a cure for venereal disease would only encourage those who suffered from it to go out and sin again.

The first reported case of venereal disease in Scotland was in 1497 in Aberdeen. Then, the connection between syphilis and sexual behaviour had not been established, but as 'licht' women, or harlots, were suspected of being the carriers, attempts to control the spread of contagion were made by controlling women's activities. Therefore, the link was made between women and dangerous diseases. The Edict of Aberdeen, issued in April 1497 by the Town Council, instituted the branding and banishment of known harlots.

In August 1497, Edinburgh issued the Glengore Act, which included the transportation of the infected to the island of Inchkeith. In case they tried to return to town, they were branded on the face.

As it was believed that venereal disease could be spread by breathing the same air as the sufferers, or even by touching them, Glasgow's drastic measures included isolation and quarantine, often in houses outside the city gates, in plague fields or in leper colonies, like Sighthill. However, according to Glasgow's burgh records, the Council made no further provision to house or treat sufferers. Actually, there's no mention of treatment for venereal disease until 1596 when Scottish surgeon Peter Lowe published a work on syphilis in which he mentioned 'an easie, certain, and perfect method to cure and prevent the Spanish Sickness'. Lowe cited, as the causes of the disease, intercourse, kissing, infected midwives, standing on infected spittle with bare feet and using an infected privy, which some people still believe can cause the disease.

While Aberdeen and Edinburgh branded those infected to show that they were reviled by God, Glasgow did not.

Although at the time there were various names for venereal disease – glengore, the sickness of Naples, the French disease and the Spanish sickness

Glasgow's Town Hospital in Clyde Street by Thomas Fairbairn

– they were all thought to be syphilis. It was not until 1793 that an Edinburgh doctor realised that there were two types of venereal disease – syphilis and gonorrhoea. The 'clap' was slang for gonorrhoea from the old French *clapoir* (a venereal sore). Edinburgh was more enlightened than Glasgow, and its Royal Infirmary opened a ward with twelve beds for both sexes suffering from venereal diseases in 1750.

When Glasgow's Town Hospital opened in Clyde Street in 1733, it did not admit anyone with venereal disease. In fact, it did not admit the sick as it was a workhouse for the 'deserving poor' until an infirmary and a lunatic asylum were added in 1740. Previously, when inmates were ill, they were attended by members of the Faculty of Physicians, Surgeons and Apothecaries, who 'furnished the sick with daily attendance, drugs and medicines, gratis'. Further building in 1766 added extra beds and extended the teaching facility for clinical instruction of medical students and surgeons' apprentices.

Although the establishment did not admit pregnant or infected women, men in the last stages of syphilis were admitted to the cells for the insane, an area that became so congested and deplorable that, by 1787, plans were made for a new hospital, the Royal Infirmary.

Glasgow's Royal Infirmary opened in 1794, as did the new army barracks in Gallowgate, holding 1,200 men. Previously, soldiers were billeted

Old postcard showing Robert Adam's infirmary which was demolished in 1912

on the inhabitants. A year after the hospital opened, wards were set aside for the treatment of soldiers, with the regiments meeting the costs. A flat rate of 8d per day was charged for each soldier admitted, with a 'fine' of 5/- for each admitted with venereal disease.

Despite the huge spread of venereal diseases in the city, caused by soldiers sleeping with the 'sporting ladies', the Royal Infirmary admitted only a few infected women and, at that, they had to prove to doctors beyond a doubt that they had contracted the disease from their soldier husbands. Only 18 women out of hundreds ever managed to do so.

Glasgow waited until the social consequences of venereal diseases had become critical before deciding to open a Lock Hospital for women. Not everybody was in favour, however, and from January to August 1805, the furious debate on opening such an establishment was reported in the *Glasgow Courier*. One faction opposed the Lock on moral and religious grounds, its perception of venereal disease being that it was God's punishment for sin, an act of God or divine retribution for the sin of venery. It also objected to medical intervention and to an establishment where women could be cured of the evil disease, enabling them to sin again. Those supporting the Lock had abandoned the 'retribution' theory for a more scientific understanding of the causes of venereal diseases. They argued that a fear of a disease could not logically be used against it and that a Christian physician had a moral obligation to relieve human suffering, no matter what caused it. Eventually, the proposal was approved, but only if a refuge or charity for reformation, such as a Magdalene Asylum for prostitutes, was established. After all, Edinburgh had one.

In 1805, the Glasgow Lock Hospital opened at 151 Rottenrow Lane (at the top of the present Montrose Street), with eleven beds and three of a staff. The prospectus stated, 'Women are often innocent victims, sinned against by errant husbands and no moral scruples should stand in the way of subscription to this new and worthy charity. The doctors who attended the hospital were not paid and did not like their involvement talked about.'

However, such was the controversy surrounding the Lock that Glasgow did not officially recognise it until 1807 when burgh records say, 'It is sincerely expected that the treatment in this place will limit the alarming spread of the evil infection.'

Until 1855, infected women could enter the Lock only with a

subscriber's line. 'Fallen women' were admitted only as part of the two-way traffic that began with the opening of the Magdalene Asylum in 1812 in Dobbies Loan, near the Lock. In other words, the 'Magdalene Asylum for Fallen Women' referred infected women to the Lock to be sent back 'as and when cured'. The Magdalene aimed at the suppression of 'the resorts of profligacy' and at the same time sought to provide 'a temporary home for females who have strayed from the paths of virtue and are willing to return to them: also a similar refuge or other protection to females who are in imminent danger of being led astray'.

By 1846, Glasgow's Lock Hospital had moved to purpose-built premises at 41 Rottenrow, with the Lock's philosophy emblazoned above the entrance – 'TREATMENT – KNOWLEDGE – REFORMATION'. The new building had seven wards and forty-five beds. Dr Lawrie, the surgeon, was to expect no remuneration.

In the first 15 months, the 'new' hospital admitted 54 patients who, although not legally under restraint, were kept in reformatory conditions. If admitted from the Magdalene, their heads would have been shaved, they would have been bathed in carbolic solutions and they would have been examined for infection. Non-referral admissions were allowed to keep their hair but were disinfected and examined. Baggy brown smocks sewn by the inmates were worn, along with regulation drawers and boots. Women from Duke Street Prison sent to the Lock remained manacled during treatment.

Although the average stay in the Lock was 29 nights, inmates were often kept there so long that they lost their jobs. Anyway, the stigma of being there in the first place meant they would have no choice when they were released but to turn to prostitution to make money.

Medical treatment was primitive – mercurial preparations, ointments and pills (found to be most effective against syphilis), salves, dressings, poultices and baths. Gonorrhoea is hardly mentioned. While the pills and potions provided slight initial relief, the mercury slowly destroyed tissue and brain cells, causing heavy salivation and sores. The mercurial vapour bath installed in 1854 sent steam into every pore, speeding up the destruction of the brain and reproductive organs.

Unlike its sister institutions, the Magdalene and the Lunatic Asylum in Cowcaddens, the Lock had no viewing gallery. Callous though it may seem, a popular Sunday pastime for ladies and gentlemen after morning church service was to gawp at the unfortunate inmates of the Magdalene and the Lunatic Asylum.

From 1846 on, the volume of applicants overwhelmed Dr Lawrie and his staff. Migrants from Highland areas and Ireland poured into an already congested Glasgow, hoping to escape from famine and grinding poverty. It was also a time when cholera and typhus raged in the city, and, when the new fever department of the Royal Infirmary couldn't cope, every available establishment was pressed into service, even the Lock despite its reputation.

As an increasing number of women, often widowed or abandoned, took to the streets to survive, street missionary work was active, with midnight meetings and the opening of refuges for the reclamation of 'fallen women'. Daily Christian services and religious instruction were started at the Lock, with compulsory attendance for inmates.

In the 1850s, Glasgow's many variety theatres and music halls employed hundreds of women, and theatre managers subscribed to the Lock to have them checked regularly. But, as those infected could be away from work for 30 days, women were often 'unavailable' for inspection.

In the Lock report of 1860, the directors issued a plea for a permanent arrangement to be made with a worthy institution for the transfer of cured Lock patients: 'No class can be more unhappily situated than the discharged of the Lock. Society has closed her portals against them with no recourse left to ensure a living other than returning to their old ways.'

In England and Ireland, pressure from the Army and the Navy led to the passing of the Contagious Diseases Acts of 1864, 1866 and 1869, their purpose being to control the spread of venereal diseases among the military and to avoid whole regiments and flotillas being 'clapped out'. As prostitutes were arrested, detained and given a compulsory vaginal examination, vociferous abolitionist movements surfaced, claiming that such an examination was 'institutional rape' and an 'invasion of a woman's person'. The women who submitted voluntarily once per month for examination and started a course of treatment were referred to as 'Government women' or 'Queen's women'.

As an alternative to the Contagious Diseases Acts, Glasgow came up with a strategy of its own, known as the 'Glasgow system' – a regime of police repression for the control of brothels and prostitution. The system, carried out over a period of ten years, was so successful that the 'Spoony Men', brothel-keepers and women moved to Edinburgh. However, when the

Glasgow system was adopted in Edinburgh in 1881, those 'in the trade' moved back to Glasgow. (Spoony Men were not pimps. They were businessmen who financed prostitutes by renting out clothes and props to them – blouses 1/- per evening, petticoats and bonnets 9d per evening.)

Chief Constable Alexander McCall, the scourge of Glasgow's prostitutes, was responsible for clearing out the city's brothels and, in the ten years that the Glasgow system was in operation, reduced them from over 300 to 22. His special constables had the power to turn women on to the streets and arrest them. Those arrested were either taken to prison or to the Lock, where they were subjected to enforced internal examinations. The streets were also cleared of prostitutes by fining and jailing. Ironically, of the 140 special constables recruited for the exercise, 67 reported sick and required treatment for venereal disease.

Although child victims of abuse and incest were being discovered in huge numbers, Victorian society preferred to pretend it didn't happen. Lock surgeon Alexander Paterson is actually on record in 1882 as saying that a seven-year-old girl 'had given the illness to herself'. Around 1890 Annie Ellen McGuire, aged nine, and Elizabeth Martin, aged seven, received treatment at the Lock for syphilis. Both girls died. They had not been born with the disease but were victims of sexual abuse. As young virgins, they may even have been used by infected men as 'cures' for syphilis, a belief popular at the time.

In the late 19th century, while most of the patients in the Lock were prostitutes, some were shop girls, mill girls, domestic servants, agricultural workers and wives of soldiers and tradesmen. During the years 1900–1910, an average of 321 patients were admitted to the Lock each year. Along with police courts and the Magdalene Asylum, the hospital was part of a general strategy of containing the dangerous sexuality of alleged prostitutes within the city. Medical isolation in the Lock was seen as the first stage in a process of moral regulation.

The beginning of the 20th century was a busy time for the Lock, where new methods of detection, like the Wassermann reaction test were being tried out. Important in 1916 was the opening of an outdoor department and a dispensary to accommodate vast numbers of new cases. The year 1924 saw the opening of a maternity ward and a children's ward, with record numbers needing help. These were epidemic years for venereal disease in

Glasgow and, from 1925, new centres opened to cope with the record number of people needing treatment. The Lock, renamed the Women's Hospital, continued to admit women and children.

By 1928, the Lock Hospital was regarded as a great teaching centre. One hundred and thirty students attended classes in the new Lecture Room and another outdoor dispensary was opened near the hospital, at the corner of Portland Street and Richmond Street.

The late 1930s were the declining years of the Lock Hospital, and although it still admitted women and children, modern medicines like penicillin ensured shorter bed-rest requirement. Lock reports show that, by 1940, the number of patients had decreased and closure was imminent. Seven years later the building's funds were transferred to the Royal Faculty of Physicians and Surgeons, which had continually served the Glasgow Lock Hospital free of charge. Ward 20 of Ruchill Hospital was set aside for women and children with venereal diseases. At the hospital, the routine ward work was done by a junior member of the medical staff who, it was stipulated, had to be female.

In 1947, the Lock building was in use as a Navy hostel and by naval medical administration for publication and propaganda on the subject of sexual health. Posters warned young men to avoid contact with 'dirty and dangerous women'.

The Lock was demolished in 1955, ending the institution for 'fallen and dangerous women', who were treated in such a humiliating and barbaric way. Through bigotry and hypocrisy, these unfortunate women were made scapegoats for the spread of venereal disease.

CHAPTER 6

A HIDDEN MANSION
Cunninghame Mansion, Gallery of Modern Art

If you ask Glaswegians if they know of any hidden buildings in Glasgow, it's almost certain they would not come up with the very visible Gallery of Modern Art in Queen Street. They would be wrong, however, because what is not apparent is that, sandwiched between its massive portico and the 130-foot-long hall, is what was the finest tobacco lord's mansion in the city and in Scotland.

The mansion was built for William Cunninghame of Lainshaw, one of the four men said to be responsible for Glasgow's sudden rise in the 18th century. The others were Alexander Speirs of Elderslie, John Glassford of Dougalston and James Ritchie of Busby. They were the chief of the famous 'tobacco lords' who carried on the main trade of Glasgow between 1740 and 1776 and bought the estates associated with their names out of the proceeds.

Cunningham, however, was the only merchant who made money out

Photograph showing quite clearly the Cunninghame mansion sandwiched between the portico of Corinthian pillars at the front and the long hall to the back

of American tobacco to survive the War of Independence. Before its outbreak, his company had the largest stock of tobacco in the kingdom, the price of which was 3d per pound. Immediately on the Declaration of American Independence, tobacco rose to 6d per pound, which is when Cunninghame's partners deemed it time to sell. Cunninghame disagreed and said they should keep it until the price went higher. When his partners said no, he asked each if he would sell at that price. When they all said yes, he told them he would buy the whole stock. He did and kept it till the price rose to 3s 6d, when he sold out, making a fortune.

From the proceeds, Cunninghame bought the estate of Lainshaw in Ayrshire and built a town mansion in Queen Street, Glasgow. During the mansion's construction, it was a favourite pastime of the citizens to inspect its progress, and when completed in 1780 at a cost of £10,000 – an immense sum then – it was described as 'the most superb urban place of residence of any in Scotland'. Standing back from the street, it had three storeys, with wings placed at right angles to the mansion and facing each other. There was a garden at the back and a large gravel area at the front. A parapet wall ran along the street, with two iron gates at the north and south ends.

Nine years later, Cunninghame was dead and his mansion was for sale, as the following advertisement shows:

> TO BE SOLD BY PUBLIC ROUP, if not sold privately, within the Tontine Tavern, Glasgow, on Wednesday 9th August next, that large and elegant dwelling house and offices and area of ground wherein they stand, containing about 4617 square yards situated on the west side of Queen Street, and fronting Ingram Street, Glasgow, belonging to William Cunninghame of Lainshaw. If it is the wish of the purchaser, payment of the price, or of any part, will be made to answer his conveniency upon satisfactory security. There is a servant waiting for showing the houses.

The purchasers were William Stirling & Sons, who used one wing as an office, the mansion itself being occupied by John Stirling till he died in 1811. It was then divided into two houses for his sons, William and George.

In 1817, the Stirling family, whose printing and dyeing business had been detrimentally affected by the depression following the Napoleonic Wars, offered to sell the mansion to the Royal Bank of Scotland. The property, described by the bank's directors as 'a most respectable office for the Royal Bank in a very desirable situation', was far closer to the bank's important clients than its existing branch.

Having purchased the mansion, the bank altered it by building a railed double stair to a new doorway, which opened on to the first floor. The stair led direct to the lobby, from which the telling room (formerly the drawing room) was entered on the left through folding doors covered with crimson cloth. On the right was the cashier's room. Other parts of the building were reserved for the cashier's residence.

During the Radical uproar of 1820, there were fears that the mob would plunder the bank, and Captain Smith's Guard of Sharpshooters was quartered in the wings for more than a week, with triple sentries at the gates. Queen Street and Ingram Street were patrolled, the bank and its garden being carefully barricaded to avoid any risk of looting. As the bank held much of the city's valuable plate and treasure at the time, it was regarded as 'The Mint' or 'The Tower' of Glasgow.

So real were the fears that the bank would be attacked that people were actually seen crying and wringing their hands and rushing to the bank to say farewell through the gates to some of the guards, as they might be slaughtered. Apparently, one of the city's venerable magistrates was seen with

Swann print showing the mansion when it belonged to the Royal Bank, who added the double stair to the front. The pillared building on the right is the Theatre Royal, the first theatre in Britain to be illuminated by gas, which burned down in 1829

tears trickling down his cheeks when he bade farewell to his eldest son, who was in the front rank of the armed sharpshooters.

In 1827, the bank sold the mansion as a new site for the city's Exchange, as the current Exchange Room in the Tontine in the Trongate was inadequate to cope with the ever-increasing number of members, owing to the rapid expansion of trade and manufacturing interests centred in Glasgow. Money was raised by subscription, and architect David Hamilton remodelled the mansion to suit its new role by adding a huge double portico of Corinthian columns supporting a cupola at the front and a large newsroom at the back on what had been Cunninghame's garden. The underwriters' room was the mansion's ballroom.

The Royal Exchange opened officially on 3 September 1829, an occasion celebrated by a grand public dinner attended by 500 gentlemen resident in or around Glasgow. Hamilton's newsroom, with its richly coffered ceiling, is Glasgow's most magnificent early-19th-century interior. From 1827, the land around the new Exchange was named Royal Exchange Square. Such distinguished figures as Louis Bonaparte, Gladstone and Dickens visited the Royal Exchange.

When the mansion was built, it was the finest town residence Scotland had seen and the architectural pride of Glasgow. Indeed, even 50 years afterwards, citizens still spoke of it as the finest urban house in Scotland and, when town planners in the 1840s proposed to pull it down to join Ingram Street and Gordon Street, such an outcry was raised that the project was abandoned.

In the building's lifetime, it has been a home, a bank, a stock exchange, Glasgow's first telephone exchange with the addition of a mansard storey in 1888, Stirling's Library and the Gallery of Modern Art.

Now that you know what you are looking for, you will have no difficulty in detecting the Cunninghame Mansion nestling between the Gallery's great portico and the long hall to the rear.

CHAPTER 7

APPEARANCES ARE DECEPTIVE
Ramshorn Church, Ingram Street

As they pass the Ramshorn Church in Ingram Street, most people think it's just another old church and walk on without paying any attention to it. What they don't know is that it's anything but just another old church, for its facade hides a theatre, one of the best collections of Victorian stained glass in Scotland and a crypt where many of Glasgow's old worthies are buried.

The proper name of the church is St David's but, because it was built on Ramshorn lands, it has always been known by the quaint name of Ramshorn, as was its predecessor, demolished to form Ingram Street. Although Ramshorn is one of the city's oldest names, its origin is obscure, with most explanations being legendary. One has it that in the days of St

Ramshorn Church façade

Mungo, a thief stole a ram from the bishop's flock and cut off its head, which instantly petrified and stuck to his hand beyond the power of removal by any means. The thief was forced to confess his sin to St Mungo, who gave him absolution and gifted the ram to him. The area where this miracle happened became known as the lands of Ramshorn.

Built in 1824, St David's is the work of Birmingham architect Thomas Rickman, who based his designs on those typical of the late 13th and early 14th centuries. St David's, Scotland's first example of the Gothic Revival, is built in the shape of a cross with a square front tower that was meant to hold 'a ring of bells' but never did. The facade and tower are decorated with embrasures and pinnacles, and the windows are ornamented with mullions and extremely graceful tracery.

Rickman was not the only person involved in designing the church. Dr James Cleland, Glasgow's Town Superintendent of Public Works, altered Rickman's plans, as he didn't like them. Taking them home, he gave strict instructions that he was to be left alone for three days to give him plenty of time to improve them. His 'improvements' included a burial crypt, partly above ground level, and a hideous neck-breaking stair people said threatened life and limb. Contemporary cartoons showed that people falling head over heels down the steps. Cleland's alterations made the church stand higher than intended.

In 1992 the church was converted into a public theatre by Strathclyde University. When the building was a church (until 1982), it was T-shaped and, to convert it into a theatre, the university used the top of the T as a foyer, its leg as an auditorium and the church halls as offices, a rehearsal room, a dressing room, a wardrobe room, etc. Although the home of the Strathclyde Theatre Group, the theatre, which can seat 150, is also used by touring

Foyer of the Ramshorn Theatre, which once held a pulpit and pews

companies. It also offers a foyer for exhibitions, social events and conferences, and is a popular venue for jazz events.

Those who are interested in stained glass are in for a treat if they visit the Ramshorn, as it contains an outstanding and varied collection, most of it produced in Glasgow and said to be 'arguably the finest Victorian stained glass in Scotland'. The city was at the time a world leader in producing stained glass and the opportunity to install it in the church came during refurbishment in 1886, when the side galleries were removed, revealing for the first time the glorious height of Rickman's Gothic Revival windows. (The biblical multi-coloured windows were extremely popular when they were displayed to the public at the end of the 19th century.) That the windows have survived is amazing as they have been removed at least three times in their life, for example, during both World Wars.

One of the magnificent stained-glass windows

There are 16 windows in the foyer, among them the Presentation of Christ in the Temple, erected by Robert Carrick Buchanan of Drumpellier in memory of his ancestors. (Buchanan Street was named after the Buchanan family, who were tobacco lords.) Another three-light window shows Abraham with a shepherd's crook, Isaac with the wood for the sacrifice on Mount Moriah, and Jacob and his staff. Above are inscriptions referring to the promises to the patriarchs: 'Surely the Lord is in this place and I knew it not (Genesis 22:18); 'I am with thee and will bless thee' (Genesis 26:24); 'In thee shall all the nations of the earth be blessed' (Genesis 22:18). When the windows were put back in place after the Second World War, the upper portions of the left and right windows were transposed – the text for Abraham is above that of the Jacob window, and vice versa.

There are 13 windows in the auditorium, three hidden from view. One of those on view is *Well Done, Good and Faithful Servant*, erected by the congregation in memory of the Rev. Robert Dickson, who died in 1903 after 23 years as minister of the Ramshorn. Another visible window is the colourful *Solomon and the Queen of Sheba*, given in memory of John Carrick who died in 1890 after 46 years as City Architect and Master of Works. Beside the main figures, a small inset shows Carrick's portrait.

At the stage end, the windows have a sloping piece of plain glass inserted among the coloured. This is where the balconies once cut across the windows, showing that the Victorians were smart not to waste money on patterned glass that would be hidden from view.

Running the full size of the foyer and auditorium, the crypt is partly above ground. It has groin vaults supported by cast-iron pillars and small Gothic-style windows (originally intended to admit light and air) that are now bricked up, making it necessary for anyone entering the crypt to take a torch, as the crypt is not wired for electricity. Although there are memorial tablets and lair numbers around the walls, all the graves are under the floor, as the walls were not deep enough for burials.

The crypt is not open to the public, as it is unsafe, and those who enter it have to mind where they put their feet, as most of the floorboards covering the graves are in poor condition. Once inside the creepy dusty chamber, difficult though it is to see anything clearly by torchlight, there's no difficulty in making out the enormous black double sarcophagus and headstone belonging to the Dalgleish family of Dennistoun.

Because of the unsafe floorboards, it is not possible to get near some of the massive, beautifully carved monuments. One lair that is accessible belongs to the family of Glasgow man Alex Broom whose daughter Janet, aged ten months, died on 29 September 1827. Her mother followed five days later.

Moving through the crypt, you will see that some tablets have vanished from the walls, leaving only the lair numbers to prove they existed. The most handsome monument in the crypt belongs to James Cleland. There are two memorials to him – the original tablet and another bearing the inscription:

FROM THE CORPORATION OF GLASGOW TO JAMES CLELAND, TO WHOSE CARE WAS COMMITTED THE ERECTION OF THIS EDIFICE, MDCCCXXV.

Apparently, the Corporation's gratitude for the successful completion of the church and other buildings by Cleland took the form of a tombstone and grave in the crypt he designed. In the opinion of many people, however, the gift was of a dubious nature and, in any case, Cleland lived for another 15 years before taking possession of it in 1840.

It's a pity the crypt is unsafe and has no lighting. Being able to see the monuments and read the inscriptions would show just how many old Glasgow worthies were buried there – many of the famous names of the city's mercantile past. The university does hope to have the crypt made safe so that the public can see round it but, until then, it's only the church that can be visited during Doors Open Day. Doors Open Day, when hundreds of interesting buildings are open free to the public, was first introduced to the UK by Glasgow Building Preservation Trust as part of the 1990 Glasgow City of Culture celebrations, with Glasgow and Ayr being the first participants.

CHAPTER 8

THE MINI PARK
Garnethill Park

It's not for nothing that Glasgow is known as the 'Dear Green Place', for, according to the Council, the city has 44 parks. The Council is wrong, however, for there are 45 parks, not 44. There is another that few people know about, the one created from a rat-ridden crater. It's the mini Garnethill Park, nestling among the tenements of Garnethill, and it came to be there thanks to the tireless Betty Brown, a resident of the area.

The story of the park goes back to 1971, when part of a tenement in Dalhousie Street had to be demolished. As the tenement was on a hill, other buildings also had to come down, which is when Betty Brown came on the scene. She approached the Council to see if it would convert the site into a kickabout area and a swing park for the children, amenities lacking in the neighbourhood. Negotiations with the Council were protracted, but after a heavy fight, Betty got what she wanted and the children had somewhere safe to play.

The children enjoyed their playground, until the building at its Rose Street end collapsed. At the time, the building was occupied by two German families, who had to be rescued from it, as the staircase had caved in. All the other occupants had been rehoused, as the structure was unsafe.

When the building was cleared away, instead of the site being levelled, a great crater was left behind. Local restaurant owners began using it as a dumping ground for their rubbish. However, as this included old food, it attracted rats, which were soon running all over the place.

A concerned Betty Brown notified the Council about the plague of rats. Despite repeated complaints, however, nothing was done. Betty then decided it was time to be a little more shrewd in her dealings with the Council. So, knowing that the Tourist Board was preparing promotional material for Glasgow as the City of Culture in 1990, she suggested that, as well as advertising that Garnethill had attractions such as the School of Art,

Scotland's first synagogue and the Tenement House, they should add that it also had the biggest rat pit in Glasgow, where large rats could be seen from 10 am onwards.

Betty's change of tactics brought results – a summons to the City Chambers to meet people from the City Planning Department and a director from the German Goethe Institut. The Institut, she was told, wanted to make a lasting gift to the city of Glasgow to celebrate its status as the City of Culture and had decided it should take the form of turning an ugly spot into a beauty spot for a community. Betty's rat pit fitted the bill perfectly.

The person commissioned to turn the rat-ridden eyesore into a beauty spot was a German environmental architect, Dieter Magnus, whose objective is to revitalise old and new city districts and to redesign squares, courtyards or gaps between buildings.

Dieter's appointment to design the park was a godsend to the Garnethill residents, for, rather than fitting it into his plans, he fitted it into the plans of the community. He listened to everything said to him and

Garnethill Park with its 'amphitheatre' in the foreground

designed the beautiful park for those who would be using it. He wanted to offer the people living in the area a stimulating everyday habitat that would be usable in a real sense as a piece of the new urban and local culture.

As the Goethe Institut was paying only Dieter's fees, the rest of the money to fund the project had to be found. Fortunately, the Council dipped into its pockets, as did some insurance companies. Scottish Homes, through Charing Cross Housing Association, put up £20,000. Betty Brown put in £250 and other residents chipped in.

The mini-park park is about the size of a football pitch and drops down about 20 feet from one end to the other. Features include a stone pyramid, a glass pavilion, picnic areas, a pergola and a hill with a slide, a tree house and a sandpit. An 'amphitheatre', which on sunny days attracts locals and lunching office workers, was formed out of old sandstone blocks and old road setts salvaged from the neighbourhood. A superb water feature tumbles down the hill between a rocky landscape, complete with space-age silver globes. Look out for the little bronze pigeons, by Shona Kinloch, on top of the lampposts.

Garnethill Park was officially opened on 26 October 1991. It is a visible and lasting result of the close partnership between Dieter Magnus and the community of Garnethill. Betty says that those who come across her park tell her it is one of the nicest wee parks outside Paris or Rome.

As well as being responsible for the creation of the park, Betty Brown started the Garnethill Multicultural Community Centre, as there was nowhere for the adults to meet other than in the launderette. (Garnethill has always housed a rich cultural assortment of people – Gaels displaced during the Highland Clearances, Irish escaping famine, Jews fleeing persecution, Poles, Italians, Indians, Pakistanis, Chinese, the list is endless.) Among the activities at the Centre in Rose Street, which is rented from St Aloysius Roman Catholic Church, are bingo, a health-action project, a Chinese operatic society and line dancing. A pensioners' afternoon tea dance is held on the first Wednesday of each month. The downstairs tearoom is not only appreciated by locals – shoppers often pop in from Sauchiehall Street. Betty claims it has the best and cheapest macaroni cheese in the city centre.

Betty Brown was voted Scotswoman of the Year in 1995 and, for her services to the community, received an OBE in 1999.

CHAPTER 9

A BIRD'S-EYE VIEW

Tolbooth Steeple, Glasgow Cross

If Glaswegians and tourists were asked which building they would most like to see inside, the answer would probably be the Tolbooth Steeple, whose studded wooden doors are always firmly shut to the public. Standing like a sentinel in the middle of the High Street at Glasgow Cross, it has an air of mystique like no other building in the city. The Tolbooth Steeple stands on its own, yet it looks as if something is missing. There is, because it is all that remains of Glasgow's late medieval Town Hall, the forerunner of the City Chambers.

A tollbooth was a very common feature in most historical Scottish

1970s photograph of Tolbooth Steeple standing like a stone policeman in the middle of High Street

burghs, and it served several purposes – as town hall, courthouse and prison. It also functioned, as its name suggests, as the place where the local tolls, customs dues and taxes were collected and stored.

In Glasgow, a tollbooth at the Cross is mentioned as early as 1454. Old records tell of 'The heid court of the burcht and citie of Glasgow being halden in the Tolbuithe thairof'. Little information is known of this structure except that documents called it 'Pretorium' and booths, or shops, occupied its street-level accommodation, the rents going towards maintaining the property and nothing else.

What appears to be the first municipal building became unsuitable and was taken down. In May 1625 the minutes of the Council record, 'They all ane voice has concludit that a number of stanes be provydit for building the Tolbooth about twa thousand pieces of hewin work.' The 'grund stane' of the new building was laid on 15 March 1626 and, eight months later, the five-storey building, complete with 126-foot-high steeple, became Glasgow's new civic centre. So pleased was the Council with the work that John Boyd, Master of Works on the job, received £100 for 'his bounteth and dilgens'. A Commonwealth visitor described the building as 'a very sumptuous, regulated, uniform fabric, large and lofty, most industriously and artificially carved from the very foundation to the superstructure, to the great admiration of strangers and is without exception, the paragon of beauty in the west'.

Unfortunately, the paragon of beauty had a defect. The entrance to the council chamber, on the floor above the street, was too small, which meant that a large outside stair had to be built, giving rise to a doggerel that was handed about to the amusement of the citizens:

'In architecture there are mistakes for ever mair,
But seldom so great as a house without a stair,
Nine windows in front, and three of them blin,
But when the Council are met, there's light aneuch within.'

The tollbooth's five floors were occupied by the Town Clerk's office, the court, the Council Hall, the Dean of Guild Hall and a prison which had a motto on its walls taken from a prison at Delft in Holland. The motto was in Latin but, translated into English, it read:

THIS HOUSE LOVES PEACE, HATES KNAVES,
PUNISHETH CRIMES, PRESERVES THE LAWS, AND
GOOD MEN HONOURETH.

Gawan Naythsmyth was appointed the first jailer at an annual salary of £2 4s 5d sterling.

The steeple, topped by a stone crown and weather vane, had seven storeys and was plain, apart from some Netherlandish strapwork ornamentation over the small windows. Of its seven floors, the first five gave access to the adjacent floors in the tollbooth proper via strong iron doors, now filled in. The Tolbooth Steeple has one of the only three remaining medieval crown spires in Scotland, the others being at King's College Chapel, Aberdeen, and St Giles' Cathedral, Edinburgh.

Records show that the earlier tollbooth contained a bell, presumed to have been installed in the new steeple, as a bell dated 1554 was known to have been there. It carried the inscription 'Kathelina-Ben-Ic-Ghegoten-Van-Jacob-Waghevns-Int-Jaerons-Heeren-MCCCCCCLIIII ('Catherine, I am cast by Jacob Wagenevesns in the year of Our Lord 1554.') The steeple also had a clock and, in 1665, a set of chimes originally intended for the steeple in the Merchants' Hall in the Briggait was installed.

The entrance to the prison, whose windows were barricaded by massive iron stanchions, was via a narrow turnpike stair in the steeple. During the day, the outer door of the entrance, which was only a half-door wicket, was guarded by a janitor, who kept his seat constantly in the passage and amused himself by looking over the half door at what was happening in the street. Beside the outside door was a strong inside door securing the entry up the narrow staircase to the prison. The janitor kept the inner door continually locked. Close to the entry was a sentry box with a soldier always on guard.

Burgh records contain few references to prison discipline in Glasgow's tollbooth but, an incident in 1666 illustrates the relations existing between the prisoners and their jailers, who had despotic powers and were often guilty of inflicting severe pain on their charges. John Rowat was the jailer at the time and one of his prisoners was the Laird of Branshoyle, jailed for some crime not stated. Rowat had some kind of dispute with the prisoner, which ended with him being put in irons. On discovering this, some of the laird's friends complained to the magistrates, who sacked the jailer. Rowat, however, applied to be reinstated, apologising profusely for having exceeded his power by putting the laird in irons although he had been highly provoked. He got his job back but lost it again soon afterwards for allowing a prisoner to escape.

Debtors were housed in the prison, and it was a daily occurrence for them to lower a shoe by a cord from the upper windows to the pavement to get coppers from sympathising passers-by. One man, anxious to see what was happening outside, squeezed his head through the bars of one of the windows and found it impossible to get it back again. The poor man's cries of distress drew attention to his ludicrous position, self-pilloried in the sight of hundreds of citizens. It took hours for him to be extricated.

Until 1790, the steeple was surrounded by iron spikes on which were once stuck the heads of those whose fate the authorities wished to proclaim to the city, such as those who adhered to presbytery during the reigns of Charles II and James VII. The spikes were pointed out to 'girning weans' as a terrific 'hobgoblin'.

From 1788 to 1813, public hangings took place in front of the steeple. During that time 21 men and one woman were hanged. When the gibbet was not in use, it was kept in the crypt of the cathedral.

A stone platform formed the base of the gallows which, on King George III's birthday (4 June), was used for a more honourable purpose. At seven in the evening the magistrates and councillors assembled on the platform to drink the health of the king. A small infantry company then fired a salute and the bells in the steeple were rung for an hour. After this there were fireworks and everyone was allowed to run riot for the remainder of the night. Another use of the platform was as a place of humiliation for lawbreakers. An offender would be sentenced to stand on it for an hour with a placard on his breast denoting his name and offence. Besides the placard, a symbol of his offence was added – a man who had stolen sacks had his head stuck through one; an unfortunate hen thief had two cocks tethered on either side of him, who, in trying to free themselves, attacked the face of the offender, much to the delight of the spectators.

By the third decade of the 18th century, the accommodation in the tollbooth had become cramped and, in 1735, the Council bought the adjoining land to build a new town hall, which opened in 1740. It had an assembly room on the ground floor, a town hall (communicating with the old tollbooth by an internal door) on the first floor and municipal chambers on the second floor.

The assembly room lay behind a broad piazza with five arches, the keystones of which were formed by a grotesque stone face carved by Mungo Naismith, the builder of St Andrew's Church.

When a syndicate that had set up a tontine in Glasgow took over the piazza'd building in 1781, it added an extension matching the existing architecture, which increased the number of arches and faces to ten. From then on, the faces were known as the Tontine Faces and became the city's most famous architectural feature.

By 1814, the tollbooth was totally inadequate as a civic centre, so the jail, court, council chambers etc., moved to new quarters at the foot of the Saltmarket, designed by William Stark.

On 14 May 1814, the tollbooth was rebuilt by architect David Hamilton in a Gothic style meant to resemble the original. Happily, the steeple was retained, although it was touch and go, as the city fathers, after weeks of consideration, agreed by a majority of only 15 votes to nine 'to

David Hamilton's Tollbooth with old steeple

preserve, support and repair the crowned tower of the old building'.

While some alterations were being made in the 1880s on the south-east corner of the rebuilt tollbooth, the workmen came across a stone-built chamber measuring about nine feet square, with neither door nor window. It was on a level with the sill of the lowest window of the steeple. As it was around the spot where the scaffold was formerly erected, it was thought that the chamber was the condemned cell and that, when the building was rebuilt in 1814, it was merely closed up and left in its former condition, as it did not seriously interfere with the rebuilding.

When David Hamilton's tollbooth was demolished in the mid 1920s, the steeple was again under threat of demolition, this time to ease the flow of traffic into the High Street. Fortunately, it was given another stay of execution, the road being widened, leaving the steeple marooned on its island, remarkably unchanged after three and a half centuries.

When the door of the Tolbooth Steeple creaks open, the smell of ancient Glasgow's history assails the nostrils. Inside the building, it's like going back in time, and it feels strange to be inside one of the oldest and most recognisable landmarks in the city.

What's surprising is that the steeple is not gloomy but quite well lit. What's also surprising is that although the exterior is square the interior is round. Inside the steeple, there are a lot of stairs, twisting but not as narrow as the building's outward appearance suggests, that is, until the top floors are reached.

On the second floor there is a grating about two feet square in the wall, covering the opening of a shaft down which the ropes from the belfry hung so that the bells could be rung from that level without the need to climb to the top. The opening is now blocked up.

The places where the old building connected with the steeple are apparent on each floor from the door outlines in the walls. Near the top there's a landing where you can see the works of the clock, which was installed in 1881 and which chimes every quarter of an hour.

Just above the clock is the hidden treasure of the tower, the little turret room from which the bells are operated by a double-row keyboard containing 16 giant handles connected by wires to the bells. The bells are rung by depressing the handles. On either side of the music stand are fittings for the candles that were used in the days before electricity.

The first musical bells were installed in 1736, and a different tune was played on each day of the week – Sunday 'Easter Hymn', Monday 'Gilderoy', Tuesday 'Nancy to the Green Wood Gane', Wednesday 'Tweedside', Thursday 'The Lass of Patie's Mill', Friday 'The Last time I Cam o'er the Muir' and Saturday 'Roslin Castle'. The present carillon of bells, consisting of one big bell and 16 smaller ones, was cast by Messrs John C. Wilson and Co., Gorbals Foundry. The big bell is inscribed 'This carillon of 16 bells, erected AD 1881'.

Beside the keyboard is a chart of those who have rung the bells, starting with Roger Redburn in 1738. At a cost of £4 3s, the Council sent Redburn to Edinburgh to learn how 'to play on the musick bells'. When Redburn died, the Council decided that the office of playing the bells should be bestowed on a person learned in the parts of music and recommended the magistrates to intimate in the public newspapers that any person skilled in playing on bells, as well as on the violin, spinet, or harpsichord, and well versed in church music, will meet with good encouragement. On 9 October 1765, Mr Collet of London was appointed to play the bells.

The present bellringer is Warren Brown, who took over in 1973 from Jessie Herbert, a member of a family whose connection with ringing the bells stretched back to 1830, when James Bayne was the bellringer. Thomas Bayne took over from 1875 until 1886, when the job passed to the female side of the

Bells and mechanism in the crown spire

family, the Herberts. Between 1886 and 1973, three generations of the Herbert family rang the bells – Thomas, William and Jessie.

The bells used to be rung daily but are now heard only on Hogmanay, when crowds gather at the Cross to welcome in the New Year. To celebrate the millennium, Warren Brown played 'Auld Lang Syne'.

From the bellringing platform there is a narrow spiral staircase up to a hatch leading to the belfry. The cast-iron staircase was installed around 1900, but in a corner are the remains of the ancient stone steps. Close up, the bells are enormous.

The long climb to the top of the steeple is rewarding, for the views are stunning – to the north, the Cathedral; to the west, Trongate; to the south, the Saltmarket; and to the east, the Gallowgate. Some landmarks from the 17th-century view of the city from the top remain – the Merchant's Steeple in the Briggait, the Tron Steeple in the Trongate and the Cathedral.

Unfortunately, it's not practical to allow the public to enter the steeple, as the stairs are much too difficult to negotiate. Therefore, citizens and tourists must be content with trying to have a look in if they pass when someone is entering the building.

View to the east from the top of the steeple showing the Mercat Cross, erected in 1930

CHAPTER 10

BEHIND CLOSED DOORS

Royal College of Physicians and Surgeons, St Vincent Street

The public can only wonder at what lies behind the doors of 232–242 St Vincent Street, as they are open only to members of Glasgow's Royal College of Physicians and Surgeons. What does lie behind them, however, is a fascinating place that, besides being of interest historically and architecturally, has a treasure trove of old surgical instruments, specimens and other medical memorabilia.

Glasgow's Royal College of Physicians and Surgeons enjoys a unique position among similar colleges in the UK in that both physicians and surgeons (including dentists) make up its membership and fellowship. Peter Lowe, a Scottish surgeon who, for about 30 years, practised in France, where he became surgeon to King Henri IV, founded it in 1599. On his return to Scotland, he had settled in Glasgow, where the state of its medical practice (which he believed

232–242 St. Vincent Street

was in the hands of 'ignorant, unskilled and unlernt personis') horrified him. In fact, it so horrified him that he petitioned King James VI for permission to establish a regulatory body to ensure that people acting as doctors (physicians and surgeons) in the city had proper training.

Early in the College's life, it passed a bye-law for a modified admission of barbers and, although in 1656 the surgeons and barbers were incorporated into a City Guild, it didn't work out and they separated in 1719.

During its long existence, the College (originally called the Faculty but changed to College by Royal assent in 1962) has had several homes. In its early days, it met in various places, including members' homes, Blackfriars Kirk and Hutchesons' Hospital. It was not until 1698 (when it was 99 years old) that it moved into its first Faculty Hall, in the Trongate, immediately to the west of the Tron Steeple. In 1791, it moved to St Enoch's Square and, in 1862, bought its present home, 242 St Vincent Street, a mansion house built around 1820 by Glasgow merchant Robert Blair. Later, adjacent properties were added, giving the College the now magnificent frontage of 232–242 St Vincent Street.

Since its foundation, the College has set high standards in medical education and training, and although from the 18th century, the Glasgow University Medical School took on undergraduate training of doctors, the postgraduate training of specialists remains a College responsibility. To meet this it has an extensive education programme, organising lectures, seminars, practical courses and workshops. In addition, as all doctors and dentists require to keep themselves abreast of developments in their particular fields, the College provides opportunities for them to update their skills and knowledge.

In its original Royal Charter, the College's members and fellows were charged with 'visiting and treating the poor, *gratis*', and although the state has now largely taken this function over, the College is still represented on charitable and philanthropic bodies in Glasgow. The Charter also empowered the College to inspect and control the drugs sold in Glasgow, a right not granted in Edinburgh until considerably later.

The first thing to catch the eye on entering the College is Sir William MacEwen's operating table, bearing no resemblance, thank goodness, to those of today, in the reception area. It's simply a narrow wooden table with end flaps that could be lowered or raised according to what the surgeon wanted. (No bloodstains are apparent on the nicely polished surface.) The table, used by MacEwen at the Western Infirmary, was found in the McKelvie Hospital,

Oban, and the Board of Management of the Oban and District Hospitals presented it to the College in May 1954. MacEwen was the greatest innovative surgeon to emerge from the Glasgow School of Medicine in Victorian times.

A ground-floor room commemorates the explorer David Livingstone, a licentiate of the Faculty who was awarded its Honorary Fellowship in 1857 on his return from the first of his travels in Africa. Memorabilia displayed include Livingstone's instrument case, correspondence and a cast of his humerus, fractured when a lion attacked him on his first journey to Africa. After his death, Livingstone's body was eviscerated, disarticulated, salted and baked in the sun before transportation to the UK, so his fractured humerus, which had not united properly, was the only means of identification, his face being unrecognisable.

The galleried Lower Library, with spiral staircases, was originally two rooms, the front looking out on to St Vincent Street and the back on to St Vincent Lane. As well as being a reading area, it is used for displays, lunches and dinners. The main Library and reading room, also home to a substantial collection of medical and other memorabilia, including early surgical instruments, is on the second floor.

Founded in 1698, when the College purchased its first building, the Library possesses many valuable manuscripts, early printed works, historical

Sir William MacEwen's operating table

medical and surgical texts, and modern books and journals. It also has the Glasgow Collection, an important extensive collection of books relating to the city's development and social/economic history. The Library's oldest books are the two 1479 printings of the *Liber Aggregatus* of Serapion the Younger and the *Brevarium* of Serapion the Elder. Both works are from the Arabic medical tradition and, despite having the same name, the authors are not known to have been related. Only two copies of the *Brevarium* are known to exist in Britain, the Wellcome Institute for the History of Medicine having the other one.

Also on the ground floor is the Lister Room, commemorating Joseph Lister, who, when Professor of Surgery at Glasgow University (1860–69), revolutionised surgery by introducing antiseptics, into the operating theatre. This room, originally the dining room of the house at 242 St Vincent Street, has dark stained wood panelling, white walls, blue marblised Corinthian columns with gilded capitals and a ceiling decorated in blue, purple and white.

The focal point of the room is the stone fireplace and tiled grate, which came from Lister's accident ward 24 in the old Royal Infirmary. Rescued by two of his pupils, Sir Hector Cameron and Professor J. H. Teacher, when his wards were demolished in 1924, they were given to the College in 1927. An interesting piece of medical memorabilia, a bleeding bowl, sits on the mantelshelf. A bronze plaque showing Lister's head was presented to the College by Sir Hector in 1909 and inserted into the fireplace's high wooden mantelpiece in 1928. The plaque is a copy of that erected in the Royal Infirmary by the staff.

Also rescued from ward 24 was a round table that is on display along with Lister's graduation gown. (Lister studied at University College, London,

The Lister Room

'the godless college', as, since he was a Quaker, establishments such as Oxford and Cambridge were closed to him.)

Directly above the Lister Room is the Alexandra Room, 242's original drawing room. Named in 1962 after Princess Alexandra of Kent, the College's first Royal Fellow (1960), the spectacular room served as the Faculty Hall until 1893, when a new one was built. Decorated in pale green with the Georgian plasterwork picked out in white, the room has a portrait of Princess Alexandra by Judy Cassab (on loan from the P & O Shipping Company) and one by Richard Foster of the late Diana, Princess of Wales, Royal Patron of the College (1983–96). Diana was the College's first Royal Patron.

At one time the fellows used the room like a gentlemen's club, and one of its valuable pieces of furniture is an antique newspaper table. It was in this room that Joseph Lister delivered a lecture on germ theory in 1868, the year after he first published on the subject in the *Lancet*. His audience was sceptical.

At the top of the main staircase is College Hall, added to the College in 1892 and designed by J. J. Burnet. Burnet's Hall is a spectacular example of late Victoriana, with its dark woodwork and high ceiling with curved beams. However, it's to the massive wooden fireplace at the western end of the room that the eye is immediately drawn. Extremely elaborate even by Victorian standards, it has marble pillars, one on either side, and woodwork heavy with carvings, such as that in the middle depicting the staff of Mercury which has two snakes twined round it. Why it should be Mercury is unclear, as the symbol of the medical profession is the staff of Aesculapius, which has only one snake twined round it. One explanation offered is that it was because Mercury's staff,

The Alexandra Room

with one side a mirror image of the other, was more symmetrical than Aesculapius', with its one snake. As the College's original insignia shows the staff of Aesculapius, it is feasible that Mercury's staff was substituted for aesthetic reasons. As with the furniture in the Hall, the famous Glasgow firm of Wylie and Lochhead made the fireplace. After the fireplace, the Hall's most magnificent feature is the vaulted ceiling, which is divided into three compartments with plaster mouldings designed in circles.

In contrast with the lavishness of the fireplace and ceiling, the magnolia walls are extremely plain, which was probably deliberate as they serve as a backdrop for the portraits of former fellows and Presidents including Peter Lowe, the founder, and James VI, the king when the College received its Royal Charter. Unlike the Alexandra Room, where the windows reach from floor to ceiling, those in the Hall start halfway up the walls. In Beaux-Arts style, they are attributed to Voisey, with whom Burnet often worked.

The room's most important piece of furniture is the plush red-velvet-upholstered President's chair, used at all formal meetings of the College and at all functions attended by the President in the Hall.

The next time Glasgow has a Doors Open Day, a visit to the Royal College of Physicians and Surgeons is strongly recommended, as it a fascinating mixture of architecture, history and medical memorabilia.

The magnificent College Hall of 1892
(Courtesy of the Royal College of Physicians and Surgeons)

CHAPTER II

TREASURES OF THE MITCHELL'S VAULTS

Mitchell Library

Authors, journalists, students, researchers and browsers who visit the Mitchell Library never fail to be impressed by its size and by the vast number of books available for reference. But what they see is only the tip of the iceberg, as, behind the public areas, the place is so huge that new members of staff need an escort to find their way round the miles of book-filled shelves. Originally, the shelving capacity of the library was designed for 400,000 volumes. Today, there are about 1,213,000 housed in a floor area seven times bigger than Hampden Park.

While the thousands of books hidden from the gaze of the public are interesting, the rarest, most fascinating treasures are kept in a strongroom in the vaults. However, as these books are some of the most valuable in the world, security has to be a top priority. The strongroom is like Fort Knox – it takes three keys and a great tug on the handle before the massive door swings open.

Once inside the room it is impossible to know where to start looking, as it's an Aladdin's cave of fascinating tomes of all sizes, most being donated to the library or bought by funds left by bequest.

Choosing at random, there is *Dante's Divine Comedy* of 1544, which is valuable, not just because of its age but because of a torn section at the top of the binding that reveals a much earlier manuscript. Nothing is known about it, except that it is a lost manuscript that was used as part of the binding of the book.

A very rare book is the Latin version of the *Nuremberg Chronicle* by Hartmann Schedel (1493), the first fully illustrated history of the world from the Creation to 1490, America not being included as it had yet to be discovered. Strangely, although the text is in Latin, the publication date is not in Roman numerals but is shown as '1493'. What is also strange is that the title page is not at the front but at the back, which was common in medieval books. The *Chronicle* contains woodcuts, some thought to be by Albrecht Dürer, illustrating the bible, ecclesiastical and civil history, maps and views of towns and cities. Particularly interesting is the fact that the Creation starts with a blank circle, which, as the universe evolves, becomes filled in until the story of Adam and Eve is illustrated in medieval fashion. There are over 1,800 illustrations.

Above the *Nuremberg Chronicle* are the 3,000 papers, dating from the 1600s to the 1930s, of the Bogles of Bogleshole, Shettleston and Daldowie, a family involved in the heyday of the tobacco trade in Glasgow. In 1774, George Bogle, who was connected with the East India Company, was the first westerner to enter Tibet, where he became a friend of the then Dalai Lama. The business world of the time also features strongly in the papers of the Dunlops of Garnkirk and in those of Daniel Campbell of Shawfield. Another important collection connected with trade includes the correspondence, circulars, petitions, etc., accumulated by Glasgow Chamber of Commerce during its first 100 years. Glasgow Chamber of Commerce, founded in 1777, was the first in the world. All the above papers are stored in acid-free cardboard boxes.

A representation of the world in the 17th century is to be found in Blaeu's *Atlas Major* of 1663 in eleven volumes, all hand coloured. The library has the French, Latin and Spanish versions, the Spanish being the rarest. Although not to scale, these maps let us see the layout of cities worldwide at that time. One volume has a map including Glasgow.

One shelf holds a set of *Dr Johnson's Dictionary of the English Language* (1755), with its famous insult to the Scots, 'oats are a grain which in England is generally given to horses but in Scotland is eaten by the people'.

Camera Work, edited by Albert Stieglitz, is a publication that the library did not at first realise was valuable. It is unusual, as it is a periodical rather than a book, containing very fine photogravure prints from between 1903 and 1915. It is a pioneering work and was a presentation copy to James Craig Annan, son of Glasgow's famous photographer, Thomas Annan. Although the photographs have since been reproduced, students come to see the originals, as they are so fine.

There are original books of Thomas Annan's series of photographs, among them *Old Country Houses of the Old Glasgow Gentry* and *The Old Closes and Streets of Glasgow,* taken between 1868 and 1871, which brought Annan world acclaim. At the time Glasgow had made a historic decision to rid itself of the privately owned disease-ridden overcrowded slums that housed most of its citizens and commissioned Annan to photograph them for posterity.

A fascinating acquisition is the *Glasgow Courant* (1715–16), the first Glasgow newspaper, which, after volume four, became the *West Country Intelligence*. The *Courant* was contemporary with the events of the first Jacobite Rebellion and the issue for Thursday 8 December to Saturday 10 December 1715 has an article by Rob Roy McGregor on the last page. No further Glasgow newspaper was issued till 1740. The library's copies of the newspaper, which start from volume two, are bound into one volume.

Beside the *Courant* is the first history of Glasgow, *View of the City of Glasgow* (1736) by John McUre. The book shows Glasgow emerging as a city proud of its history and traditions.

A drawer holds miniature books so tiny that five of them fit into the palm of a hand. Among them are bibles with built-in magnifying glasses, a collection of Burns' poetry and the smallest book in the world, *Old King Cole*, printed by the Gleniffer Press, Paisley, in 1985. It's 1 centimetre square and has one word per page. Only 85 were printed.

From the smallest books to the largest – four volumes of John

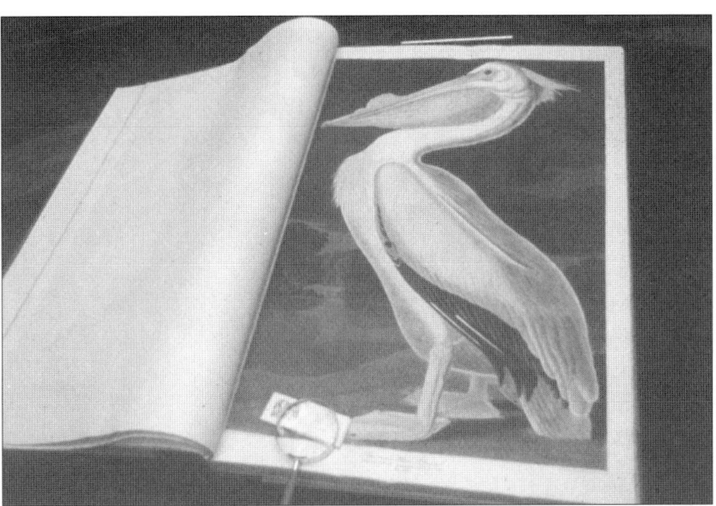

From the sublime to the ridiculous – an illustration from one of the largest books in the library, a white pelican from John Audubon's Birds of America *and at the foot of it one of the library's smallest books*

Audubon's *Birds of America* (1827–38), containing 435 hand-coloured plates. Each page measures 39 inches by 27 inches, showing the life-sized illustrations of fabulous birds, including the American white pelican, which is startlingly lifelike. American ornithologist and artist, Audubon spent years travelling all over the USA, drawing birds. However, he acquired most of his subjects by shooting them. There were no cameras and he never worked from specimens from the taxidermist's art. They had to be live or newly killed. The first to publish Audubon's work was Lizars of Edinburgh. After producing the first ten plates, however, their colourists went on strike and the remainder were published in London by Robert Havell and Son. The four volumes of *Birds of America* are enormous in value as well as size. At auction on 11 March 2000, one set established a world record for a printed book by being sold for $8.8 million – £5 million.

A locked cabinet yields treasures like *The Defence of the Augsburg Confession (1530)* by Philipp Melanchthon. What's important about this book is that it belonged to Martin Luther and is signed by him on page 2. Luther was a friend of Melanchthon.

There are also three *Books of Hours* – devotional books for the laity. The oldest is from the late 14th century, for use in the diocese of Rodez, with text in Provençal and Latin. Then comes one in Dutch from the middle of the

/ Martinus Luther

Aller durchleuchtigſter / Grosmechtigſter / Vnuberwintlichſter Keiſer / Allergnedigſter herr / Als ewer Keiſerliche Maieſtet kurtz verſchiener zeit / einen gemeinen Reichstag alhie gen Augſpurg gnediglichen auſgeſchrieben / mit anzeig vnd ernſtem beger / von ſachen / vnſern vnd des Chriſtlichen namens erbfeind / den Türcken betreffend / vnd wie dem ſelben mit beharlicher hülff ſtatlichen widerſtanden. Auch wie der zwieſpalden halben jnn dem heiligen glauben / vnd der Chriſtlichen Religion gehandelt müge werden / zu rathſchlagen / vnd vleis anzukeren / alle / eins iglichen gutbeduncken / opinion vnd meinung zwiſchen vns ſelbſt jnn lieb vnd gütigkeit / zuhören / zuerſehen / vnd zuerwegen / vnd die ſelben zu einer einigen Chriſtlichen warheit zu bringen vnd zuvergleichen / alles / ſo zu beiden teilen / nicht recht ausgeleget / oder gehandelt were / abzuthun / vnd durch vns alle / ein einige vnd ware Religion anzunemen vnd zu halten / vnd wie wir alle vnter einem Chriſto ſind / vnd ſtreitten / Alſo auch alle / jnn einer gemeinſchafft / kirchen / vnd einigkeit zu leben. Vnd wir die vnden benanten / Chürfurſt / vnd Fürſten / ſampt vnſern verwanten gleich andern Chürfurſten / Fürſten / vnd Stenden dazu erfordert / ſo haben wir vns darauff dermaſſen erhaben / das wir ſonder rhum / mit den erſten hieher komen.

Vnd als denn auch Ewer Keiſer. Maie. be-
AA ij   ruts

The page of The Defence of the Augsburg Confession *of 1530 that shows Martin Luther's signature as the book belonged to him*

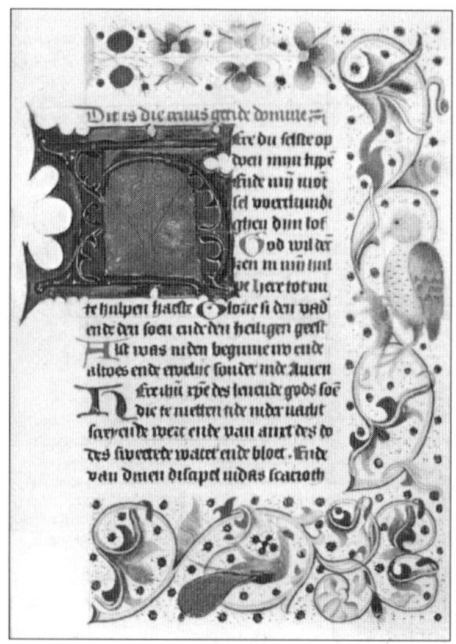

Dit is die [...] domine
Here du selste op doen mijn lippe ende mijn mont sel voertkundighen dijn lof. God wil dẽken in mijn hulpe here tot minte hulpen haeste. Glorie si den vader ende den soen ende den heiligen geest. Alst was in den beghinne nv ende altoes ende ewelijc sonder inde. Amen. Here ihũ xpẽ des levenden gods soẽ die te mettẽ tide inder nacht gevangen were ende van anxt des doodes sweetende water ende bloet. Ende van dinen discipel iudas scarioth

Leaf from the 15th-century Dutch Book of Hours *from the Cowie Collection*

15th century, and one from Rouen from the end of that century, with the main text in Latin and the calendar at the beginning in French. The books from Rodez and Rouen are vividly illuminated with miniature biblical scenes, bordered by flowers, fruit, birds and grotesque animals. Although colourful, the Dutch book is less elaborate.

Also in the cabinet are two original 1786 Kilmarnock editions (chiefly in the Scots dialect) of Burns' poetry and some of his original letters and manuscripts. Originally the Kilmarnock edition was issued as a paperback to cut costs. Only 612 copies were printed. Page 138 has 'To a Mouse'. An original Kilmarnock edition has 'Kilmarnock', the place of publication, printed on the title page. If the spine says 'Kilmarnock Edition', it is not an original. Of the two Mitchell copies, one is unique in that it was owned by a friend of Burns, Robert Aird, and where Burns left blanks or gave an initial, he wrote in the names of the persons Burns was referring to, as he knew who they were.

One of the original Burns' manuscripts owned by the library is 'Auld Lang Syne'. There are only six copies, three in Scotland, three in the USA. Burns' writing is very easy to read. In this version he wrote 'my jo' rather than 'my dear'.

The Burns' items, the *Books of Hours* and the *Augsburg Confession* belong to the Cowie collection, donated to the library in 1965 by Mrs John Cowie. Her father-in-law, Charles Rennie Cowie, was described in 1918 as 'the most outstanding Burns man in Glasgow'.

A small green box holds a Bible allegedly used by Dr Edward William Pritchard, the last man to be publicly hanged in Glasgow (28 July 1865). Pritchard poisoned his wife and mother-in-law and, because of the fake tears he shed over his wife's coffin, was known as 'the human crocodile'. The inscription inside the Bible is thought to be by one of Pritchard's jailers.

Page 1,516 of John Gerard's *Herball or Generall Historie of Plants* contains the first illustration of a banana, the text confirming that the name came from Guinea, or Ginny as it was spelt in 1633. According to the book, bananas grew on Adam's Apple Tree. The cover of the book is a late-19th-century piece of needlework.

There's a fascinating book of original photographs of Sherman's campaign in the American Civil War. Taken by George N. Barnard, they include scenes of the occupation of Nashville, the great battles around Chattanooga and Look Out Mountain and the Atlanta campaign, which shows the city to be sparsely built, with wooden buildings, one a billiard saloon. The Atlanta shots include soldiers on guard and the railyard looking slightly different from the way it is shown in *Gone With the Wind*.

From Atlanta to the Kelmscott Press An edition of the *Works of Geoffrey Chaucer* (1896), with illustrations by Edward Burne-Jones and typeface and design by William Morris was the greatest achievement of the Kelmscott Press, set up by Morris, and is a stunningly successful attempt to emulate the virtues of medieval printing.

The hand of friendship in the face of adversity is shown by the *Leningrad Album*, an album of drawings, watercolours, printed pictures, photographs and messages of greeting in Russian with English translations. This dates from 1942 and the Siege of Leningrad, when a group of women from Coatbridge and Airdrie sent messages of goodwill to the women of Leningrad. The album is the impressive and moving response from the women of Leningrad.

A whole cabinet is devoted to the drawings of William Simpson, known as 'Crimean' Simpson because of his work during the Russo–Turkish war. His sketches, which accurately represented the events, were sent to Queen Victoria, who gave him royal favour. In 1866, he became war correspondent to the *Illustrated London News*, a position he held until he retired. Among the events Simpson covered for the paper was the opening of the

The Kelmscott Chaucer

Suez Canal and the Franco-Prussian war of 1870–71.

While few of the drawings and watercolours owned by the library depict Simpson's work as a war correspondent, they do show a variety of subjects including architectural and archaeological features, figures, costumes and scenes of the countries he visited. They also show the wonderful drawing, exquisite colour and careful attention to detail he put into his work.

Over 100 Simpson items, including a few manuscripts, catalogues of his exhibitions, scrapbooks and drawings were purchased in 1912 for £114 with money from the Moir Fund. The Moncrieff Mitchell donation in 1950 included Simpson watercolours of Glasgow. *India Ancient and Modern* contains a series of vibrantly coloured illustrations of the country and people of India, which Simpson produced during the three years he spent there after the Indian Mutiny of 1857.

There are various books of photographs in the room, including those taken by Andrew Brown, Clerk of Works at the time that the Mitchell Library was built. He photographed each step of the work and, after fire had destroyed part of the dome in 1996, his photographs were referred to during the restoration work. There are also important photographs and architectural drawings by Alexander 'Greek' Thomson, donated by his granddaughter in 1934.

A grey box holds the oldest item in the Mitchell Library Collection – a 12th-century psalter containing the psalms of David in Latin. It belonged to Walter Stirling of Stirling's Library fame and is decorated with gold leaf.

Many more of the Mitchell's treasures can be seen in the Jeffrey Room at the top of the building. Cotton and linen magnate, Robert Jeffrey left his library and the funds to house it in a special room in the Mitchell in 1902. The collection contains standard works of the 19th century, like first editions of Dickens and Thackeray. It is also rich in Scottish history, particularly in works on Mary, Queen of Scots. There is also a panoramic view of *The Funeral Procession of the Duke of Wellington*. It measures four inches wide and folds out to over 60 feet, showing each stage of the spectacle.

It would be easy to go on and on about the treasures of the Mitchell, as they are so outstanding. However, those items mentioned are among the rarest and most valuable in the world and, although, for reasons of security, they cannot be put on view to the public, just to know they belong to the Mitchell and therefore to the city of Glasgow is a consolation.

CHAPTER 12

SCOTLAND'S FIRST SYNAGOGUE

Garnethill Synagogue

The interior of Garnethill Synagogue is, beyond doubt, one of Glasgow's hidden treasures. Stout shoes and lots of stamina are necessary to visit it, however, as it is situated at the top of Hill Street, a treacherous slope beginning at Sauchiehall Street.

Garnethill Synagogue, Scotland's first custom-built synagogue, was built to house the Glasgow Hebrew Congregation. Romanesque-cum-Byzantine in style, with Moorish touches, it was designed by local architect John McLeod in consultation with Nathan Solomon Joseph, architect of London's Bayswater synagogue. Benjamin Simons laid the foundation stone in March 1877, and Rabbi Dr Hermann Adler consecrated the completed

Façade of the synagogue on Renfrew Street

Interior of Prayer Hall showing the Holy Ark

building on 9 September 1879.

Carved in Hebrew in the stone above the main entrance doorway in Garnet Street is Deuteronomy 32:12, which, translated into English, is 'God alone led him and there was no strange god with him.' The numerical value of the Hebrew letters used in the verse add up to the date of the foundation of the building.

The shape of the synagogue, with its body lying at right angles to the entrance, was determined by the need for it to face east towards Jerusalem, as all British synagogues do, and to build around the house already on the site, which the congregation purchased along with the land.

The entrance hall has memorials to those who have given long and considerable service to the synagogue, such as the first minister, the Rev. E. P. Phillips, who served the congregation from 1879 to 1929. Another memorial is to the Rev. Isaac Hirshow, Reader (a cantor). He was the first music graduate of Glasgow University and, if any music graduates don't like the colour of their gowns, he is to blame, since he had the privilege of choosing it. Hirshow was minister of the congregation for 37 years.

Access to the inner hall is through a fabulous Moorish-style archway with Hebrew lettering across it, which, translated into English, is 'Blessed is he who comes in the name of the Lord,' a standard Hebrew greeting. Apparently, the Moorish design elements date from the Middle Ages, particularly from Spain before the Inquisition, when Christians, Jews and Muslims lived together in harmony, all contributing from their own cultures.

From the inner hall access is gained to the Prayer Hall and the ladies' gallery, reached by a staircase branching to right and left. The stunning stained-glass window on the staircase half-landing is one of the finest examples of stained glass in the world. The intricacy of the flower design and the vibrancy of the colours are breathtaking. Unlike in other places of worship, the windows in the synagogue have no religious significance. There are also no statues, pictures or icons in the building, as the third commandment about not worshipping idols is taken very seriously.

The Prayer Hall, which can seat 500 worshippers, has a barrel-vaulted ceiling, a gilded metalwork gallery, pillars, arches and a fabulous stained-glass dome. The focal point, however, is the Holy Ark (Aron Kodesh) set in an apse in the east wall, facing Jerusalem. The Ark, an ornate cupboard, houses the Torah scrolls, in which the five books of Moses are handwritten on parchment, exactly as Moses wrote them thousands of years ago. Because the scrolls contain the word of God, where they are kept is the most revered part of the synagogue. Scrolls are handwritten, and every scroll in every synagogue is identical. Garnethill has five that are usable and some that are not.

The letters in the scrolls are all consonants; there are no vowels. Although the scrolls are said to be read, they are, in fact, chanted, the cantellation being indicated above the letters, which read from right to left. For those not clever enough to read the scrolls, a prayerbook gives the English translation alongside the printed Hebrew words, which have vowel signs underneath as well as the cantellation. So, if the minister makes a mistake, those following the service with the prayerbook shout out and he has to start at the beginning of the sentence. All five books of Moses are on each scroll, beginning with the Book of Exodus and ending with the Book of Deuteronomy.

Although archaeologists found many of the 2,000-year-old Dead Sea Scrolls to be a mystery, one of the oldest, a large part of the Book of Leviticus, could be taken and fitted into its place in the Torah, as it is identical. Apparently, the difficulty with the other scrolls is that they have not been read for 2,000 years, unlike the Torah, which is read every week in every synagogue. There is, therefore, no problem with the vowel sounds not being there. But, with 2000-year-old scrolls that no one has read or seen, and of which all that is known is the consonants, it is almost impossible to translate them.

In front of the Ark, there is a pulpit, which was an addition, the Jewish tradition being one of teaching rather than preaching. This being the western world, however, it was decided that there was no reason why a minister or rabbi should not go into a pulpit and preach to the congregation. Above the pulpit is the Ner Tamid, an everlasting light in remembrance of the light of the temple in Jerusalem. It also serves to point out that a synagogue is not a temple. 'Synagogue' comes from a Greek word meaning 'meeting place'. Therefore, it's a place for Jews to meet, not only for prayer but also for study and even for entertainment.

In addition to the pulpit, there's a raised platform with a desk (the bimah) from which the service is conducted by the reader, or cantor. At the appropriate time, the scrolls are taken out of the Ark and placed on the reader's desk for him to read. The bimah is in the middle of the synagogue, with the congregation all around it to signify that everyone in the congregation is equal. There is, however, one inequality in Orthodox Judaism – men sit downstairs, women upstairs in the gallery. Something not normally seen in a place of worship – a clock – explains this.

A clock is very important in a synagogue, as prayers are said three times a day, seven days a week – morning, afternoon and evening. The morning prayer cannot be said until a hand can be seen in front of the face, a difficult concept in modern times, with street lighting, etc. However, 3,000 years ago in the Middle East that was the yardstick for saying morning prayers. The evening prayer is said when three stars can be seen in the sky. Working out the timings for the afternoon prayer is complicated. Afternoon is the middle of the day and depends on the length of the day, which is obviously longer in summer than in winter. Nowadays, timetables are written to give prayer times.

We now come to the reason for women sitting upstairs. Men come to pray at appointed times, which are different at different times of the year. Women do not for various reasons, such as not being able to leave a baby or a sick child to go to the synagogue. Therefore, so as not to disturb the men at prayer, women sit separately. The gallery in this synagogue is particularly ornate.

Services are conducted in Hebrew, with two exceptions, the prayer for the Royal Family, inscribed on the left of the east wall, and the prayer for the state of Israel, inscribed on the right. These are not in Hebrew as it is considered important that everyone should know them, particularly the prayer for the Royal Family. This is because Jews have been immigrants in various countries since the dispersion from Israel and have always paid proper respect to the leaders of the countries they settled in.

By any standards, the architecture and decor of the Prayer Hall are magnificent. The colour scheme is blue and yellow – walls yellow, barrel-vaulted ceiling blue with white plasterwork. Octagonal piers with ornate Byzantine capitals carry the gilded ladies' gallery and an arcaded tier supports the ceiling. There are stained-glass windows in the north and south walls, and, high on each side of the east wall, is a round window echoing the design of that on the staircase. A star of David decorates the west wall, along with a plaster plaque taken from an old place of worship in George Street. The numerical value of the Hebrew lettering on the plaque adds up to the date when the old synagogue was consecrated.

The handful of Jews who became the Garnethill Hebrew congregation first worshipped in a rented room in High Street in 1825. In 1857, a flat in George Street at the corner of John Street was converted into a synagogue, and in 1875, the congregation bought a site to build a synagogue for the increasing Jewish population, about 700 at the time. Building it cost £16,000. Refurbishing it 119 years later cost £650,000, £48,000 being spent on the fabulous stained-glass dome above the Ark, which has square panes patterned in blue and yellow, the colours alternating – one pane blue with yellow, the next yellow with blue, and so on. One pane has the first two Hebrew words of each of the Ten Commandments written on it. Another says, in Hebrew, 'Remember before whom you stand.'

Apart from the internal refurbishment and repairs to the stained glass, work on the synagogue, which is a listed building, included a new roof, extensive stone repairs and a state-of-the-art central-heating system. Using original materials and skilled craftsmen, it took two years to restore the building to its former glory. However, in the end, it was worthwhile, as today the synagogue is beautiful without being ostentatious.

The refurbishment money came from various sources – Historic Scotland, Lottery Heritage, Glasgow City Council, Glasgow Jewish Community Trust, the Wolfson Foundation and synagogue members themselves. Even the Scottish Churches Architectural Heritage Trust contributed £3,000. Dr Jonathan Sacks, the Chief Rabbi, rededicated the synagogue on 8 February 1998.

Justification for refurbishing the synagogue at such great cost is that it is believed it will become a Museum of Judaica, since the Scottish Jewish Archives Centre, established in April 1987, is housed in the building. Almost 1,500 people, Jews, non-Jews interested in Judaism, students, youth groups, pensioners groups, church groups and schoolchildren visit it each year.

The fact that the synagogue has survived so long in the city centre is remarkable, as the usual life-span of a city-centre synagogue in Europe is 60 years. After that, people move on, which means that city-centre synagogues have a very difficult time, especially since members are supposed to walk to services on the Sabbath and many now live in the suburbs. Garnethill keeps going because the founding families have preserved it from oblivion.

Despite the climb to reach it, a visit to Garnethill Synagogue on Doors Open Day is recommended, because, apart from providing an insight into Judaism, the interior of the building is beautiful.

CHAPTER 13

LOOKING DOWN
Pavement Carvings

It is said of Glasgow that much of its glory is hidden because the statuary and carving on the city's buildings require people to look up. While that is true, looking down can reveal more secrets, such as the carving in the pavement in Candleriggs, an area that got its name because of the candle factories once located there. When a fire in 1652 destroyed one-third of Glasgow, the Council banished dangerous trades from within the city. Four candle factories were therefore relocated to just beyond what was then the city's western boundary. Candleriggs was the new name given to the area – 'candle' for the candleworks and 'riggs' for the ridges of croft lands on which they had been built.

In 1675, Mungo Cochrane set up one of the city's earliest public bowling greens in Candleriggs, where it remained until 1817, when the Candleriggs Bazaar was built on the site. The Bazaar traded fruit and vegetables and, by 1914, had become the main wholesale fruit-and-vegetable market in Scotland. Congestion by horse-drawn carts and then lorries caused major obstructions in the neighbourhood, and in 1969 the market moved to Blochairn. Other businesses also moved, resulting in the area declining rapidly, with many buildings being left empty and deteriorating.

Artwork carved in the pavement in Candleriggs

As part of Glasgow's City Centre Millennium Plan, a regeneration of the Candleriggs area, begun in 1995 and finished in 1998, created a superbly reworked streetscape, the finishing touch being the pavement outside the City Halls, which was decorated with artworks carved into the surface. The panels are interpretations of Glasgow themes by sculptor Frances Pelly and the poems are by the Glasgow-based poet, Edwin Morgan.

One poem represents the 14 incorporations of the Trades House:

Fourteen heavy hammermen
Thirteen cork-heeled cordiners
Twelve well-read weavers
Eleven blistered baxters
Ten toty tailors
Nine maroculous maltsters
Eight cock-a-hoop coopers
Seven sinewy sawyers
Six sticky skinners
Five fiery fleshers
Four sturdy stonemasons
Three blossoming bonnetmakers
Two godly gardeners
One bonny barber

Paving stone inscribed with a cross with the initials R.F. and A.F., which mark the grave of the Foulis brothers

Another place to look down for hidden Glasgow is outside the Ramshorn Church graveyard in Ingram Street, where, inscribed on a paving stone, is a cross with the initials R.F. and A.F. These mark the graves of the famous printers, the Foulis brothers. The graveyard once covered all the ground right to the other side of Ingram Street and, when the street was widened, the graveyard became part of it. Passers-by for over 200 years have been unaware that they were walking over graves.

Robert and Andrew Foulis were printers who produced work that matched the finest in Europe. They had studied at Glasgow University and were booksellers before becoming printers. Although both were involved in the printing business, it was Robert who started it by purchasing a printing press equipped with both Greek and Latin type and successfully applying in 1743 to become printer to the university.

When Robert decided to publish an 'immaculate' edition of works by the Roman poet Horace in 1744, he employed six experienced proofreaders to make sure there would be no typographical errors. As a further safeguard, after the proofreaders finished, the pages were hung on a board in the university and a reward of £50 was offered to anyone who could find an error. To allow plenty of time for mistakes to be discovered, the proofs were left on the board for two weeks. Nevertheless, despite being vetted so carefully by so many, when the great work was published, there were at least as many errors as the number of proofreaders, one error being in the first line of the first page.

Shortly after the publication of Horace, Andrew joined Robert in the business and together they produced many splendid editions of Greek and Latin classics. Their superb Homer in four volumes, issued in 1756–58, has been claimed as one of the most beautiful editions ever printed. Each sheet was read and corrected six times before being printed. Their *Iliad* was the finest classic ever produced at any press. In fact, the works from the Foulis press were unsurpassed for beauty of typography and correctness of printing.

Robert Foulis was also interested in art and, when he had the idea in 1751 of setting up an academy of fine arts in Glasgow to teach painting, sculpture and engraving, he and Andrew went abroad to find teachers and to purchase pictures, casts and engravings for students to copy.

When the Glasgow Academy of Fine Arts opened in 1753, it predated the Royal Academy of Arts in London by 15 years. It was the first real attempt to foster art in Scotland and was Glasgow's first school of art. The university made several rooms available for classes and a hall for exhibitions. Robert was even given the run of the Duke of Hamilton's galleries for examples of famous pictures to copy, such as the most famous picture in Scotland, the life-size *Daniel in the Den of the Lions*.

At first, the academy attracted and nurtured great talents, and promising students were sent abroad to study at its expense. As running the academy was enormously expensive, Robert constantly sought patronage and subscriptions for financial support. Despite wealthy patrons, such as John Glassford and Provost Archibald Ingram, however, the scheme was disastrous and the academy closed in 1775. Glasgow was not ready to cultivate the arts. The efforts of the Foulis brothers were premature and there was no further attempt to cultivate art in the city until the early 19th century.

Although the academy failed, ruining the Foulis brothers, it produced students who became famous – William Cochrane, the portrait painter, David Allan, the 'Scottish Hogarth', and James Tassie, the modeller. The academy also produced some unique local views, including one showing the students hard at work in the fore hall of the university. Another shows the great fête held in the inner quadrangle on 22 September 1761, the coronation day of George III. The walls of the quadrangle are hung with pictures, among them just to the east face of the tower, the famous Rubens belonging to the

Fine art exhibition in court of Glasgow College

Duke of Hamilton. An exhibition was held on the king's birthday every year, which was the original of all our modern picture exhibitions.

Andrew Foulis died in 1775 and, a year later, Robert died while on his way home after the disappointing result of the sale of his art collection in London, which, after expenses, raised only 15/. Contrary to the advice of James Christie, the famous auctioneer, Robert sold his collection in an already glutted market, realising only 2s 6d for some items when he had expected £20.

Although it was unfortunate that the desire to cultivate the arts in Scotland ruined the brothers, Robert Foulis could be proud of starting the first school of liberal arts in Great Britain.

When someone who knew of the existence of the graves of the Foulis brothers noticed in 1925 that a trench had been cut through them for the laying of an electric cable, he notified the Town Clerk, who discovered that the contractor was unaware that part of the pavement covered what had been a graveyard. Human remains were found and re-interred but, unfortunately, during the absence of the workmen, they were dug up by a gang of youths and scattered over the surface. They were, however, again collected and re-interred. Since then, the bones of the Foulis brothers have remained at peace.

CHAPTER 14

GLASGOW'S LEAST-KNOWN MUSEUM

Strathclyde Police Museum, Pitt Street

Hidden in the bowels of the Strathclyde Police headquarters at 173 Pitt Street is not only Glasgow's best-guarded museum but its least known. It's the Strathclyde Police Museum, and it is least known possibly because it is not open to the public except by appointment or on Doors Open Day. The museum is a treasure trove of exhibits that document over a century of law and order, from old-fashioned sleuthing to the latest scientific forensic tests. It details the history of Glasgow's police force, established in 1800 and believed to be the oldest in Britain, since it precedes the London Metropolitan force by 29 years.

Before the establishment of the police force, the duty of 'watch and ward', that is, the maintenance of peace and good order, was the responsibility of the citizens. Attempts had been made in 1778 and in 1788 to set up a regular police force, but the people did not want to pay for its upkeep. The idea in 1788 was to have a municipal police force controlled by commissioners elected from among the tradespeople and merchants. Most of the proposals the magistrates came up with are still valid today. The police would have a uniform and swear an oath. They would patrol the streets in shifts 24 hours a day. They would deter thieves by concentrating on the receivers of stolen property – without the people to buy stolen goods, the market for the thieves would be diminished. They were also to keep an eye on the taverns where criminals hung out. All the proposals can be read in the handwritten minutes in the Mitchell Library.

Glasgow's plans for policing ended up in London, courtesy of Patrick Colquhoun, Glasgow's Lord Provost and founder of the Chamber of Commerce. He had moved south as a magistrate in 1789. Six years later, he wrote a book on how the London police could be improved, using the proposals put forward in Glasgow. His work inspired the setting-up of the

Thames River Police in 1800 and the Metropolitan force in 1829.

In 1789, Glasgow appointed a Master of Police, with eight constables under him. This system, however, lasted only a year when, once again, the people didn't want to pay for it. A rearrangement of the old system was then tried whereby the city was divided into four districts and all male citizens between the ages of 18 and 60 who paid rents over £3 had to take guard duty by rotation, 36 being on patrol every night, nine in each district. A tour of duty could be escaped on payment of 2s 6d for a substitute.

Meanwhile, the population was increasing rapidly and the lawlessness in the city made the inhabitants change their minds about paying for a police force. Accordingly, the Council applied for an Act of Parliament to establish a police force and to undertake the paving, lighting and cleansing of the streets.

City merchant John Stenhouse became Master of Police at a salary of £200 per annum. Also appointed were three sergeants at £40 each, six police officers at £30 each and 68 watchmen at 10s a week each. To pay for the police force, taxes were levied.

The Tron Kirk Session House became a police station, and it was there on the night of 15 November 1800 that the Glasgow police force first mustered. Commissioner Dr John Aitken described the occasion as follows:

> Our impression was that this force was so large and overwhelming that it would drive iniquity out of the city as though by a hurricane. Greatcoats and staves were served out, the latter being four feet long and chocolate brown in colour. Each watchman was given a number which was painted on the back of his greatcoat between the shoulders in large white letters.

While the only article of uniform supplied to the watchmen was a greatcoat, officers and sergeants received a blue coat with matching vest and knee breeches, an outfit identical to civilian clothing except that the seams were welted over with red stripes. Both ranks wore tall hats, and sergeants were distinguished from police officers by shoulder knots of red-and-blue-mixed worsted thread.

At first, headed by officers, watchmen patrolled the streets in squads of about a dozen. Within weeks, however, beats were introduced, when watchman were issued with a rattle, a lantern and two candles – one lighted, the other in reserve. Officers were divided into three divisions, each consisting of a sergeant and two officers. One division was on duty in the office for 24 hours, one was on patrol duty for the same period and one rested for twenty-four hours. Watchmen were on duty from 10 pm to 6 am in winter and from 10 pm to 4 am in summer. Policing the city was not their only duty. They called out the hours and the state of the weather and, until 1804, swept the streets.

As most of the watchmen were elderly, each had a sentry box to rest in if he felt tired or the weather was bad. However, as there was no regulation to prevent all the watchmen being in their boxes simultaneously, many a snooze was taken in these retreats while the city took care of itself. (At first, policemen really were watchmen, and when there was trouble a 'civic guard' was called out to maintain order.)

To mark the bicentenary of the City of Glasgow Police Act of 30 June 1800, a commemorative plaque was unveiled on 30 June 2000 at the Tron Theatre, the building where the police first mustered on 15 November 1800, then known as the Tron Church or Laigh Kirk. The City of Glasgow Police stood down on 15 May 1975, on the formation of Strathclyde Police.

A tour of the museum starts with photographs of the chief constables of Strathclyde Police, formed on 16 May 1975. Alongside are information boards showing the make-up of the Strathclyde force, blue headings indicating which were police forces and constabularies in their own right before the amalgamation.

Beside the information boards are portraits of former chief constables, the one with his hand on his chin being Sir Percy Joseph Sillitoe, Glasgow's most innovative chief constable, who came to the city from Sheffield in 1932. Sillitoe rationalised the force, cleared the razor gangs and brought in vehicles equipped with radio sets that could receive and transmit messages. He also introduced a new signal-box system and started a finger-

'Drunks barrow'

printing records office. A further introduction was something adopted worldwide and still with us – the black-and-white-diced cap band, known as the 'Sillitoe tartan'. He wanted something that would stand out and say to people, 'This is a police officer, not some other hat-wearing person like a fireman, a security guard, or a chauffeur.' His inspiration for the design is thought to have come from the cap band of the Royal Scots regiment.

Below the portraits is the first mode of police transport – the 'drunks' barrow', used until 1920. Drunks were placed face down on it with their head hanging over the front, for two reasons – if they were sick they would not choke on their vomit and it saved officers having to clean the barrow. So that they would not fall off, the drunks were strapped into the barrow. After the drunks' barrow came the horse-drawn van for prisoners, in use from 1880 to 1911.

Beyond the drunks' barrow, there is a collection of batons, going back to when the city had individual forces. Some have crests and some are so highly decorated that they were obviously used only for ceremonial purposes. Others are plain and well used. Below the batons is a cutlass that belonged to Calton Burgh Police. As Calton was a very wild area, its policemen were issued with cutlasses, not batons. Apparently, a Calton grave-robber almost had an arm severed by a cutlass blow when two officers surprised a gang violating Calton burial ground. A cutlass was issued to the City of Glasgow officers only if there was rioting.

Alongside an old sergeant's uniform is early police equipment, including a strange-looking object consisting of a thin leather strap joined to a wooden handle. This is a 'snitcher', the first form of handcuffs. The officer tied the leather tightly round his prisoner's wrists and held on to him by the handle. Before, all

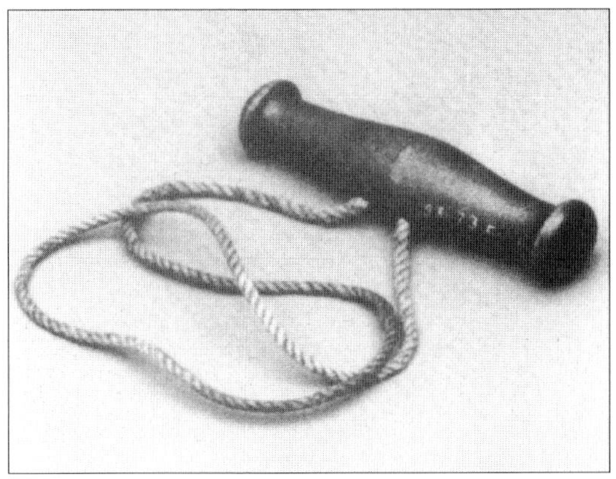

Snitcher – first form of handcuffs

the officer could do was to hold on to the criminal by hand. There is also a toughened leather neck collar worn by officers underneath the high uniform collar for protection against the razor gangs that were rampant at the time.

The section FROM FIREARMS TO FORENSICS relates to crime and to the methods used in solving it. The case of Peter Manuel, hanged for murdering seven people between 1956 and 1958, features, as does the Allison Street shooting on 30 December 1969, when three police officers were gunned down in cold blood. Two died and one was so badly injured that his life was in danger for several days.

On the weapons side, there is the knife used in one of Glasgow's most brutal and cold-blooded murders, that of Emma Dufour, who, on 24 January 1962, was found at home, her face and head struck with an iron bar and her throat cut with a bread knife. One shilling and fourpence had been stolen.

There's also the dagger used by Joseph Thomson to murder his wife on 16 March 1927. She had been found with her throat cut and a dagger thrust into her breast. At Thomson's trial, a special plea of insanity was lodged, as he was incapable of instructing his defence. The court heard that in a letter he wrote to his mother before the murder he stated, 'in the cupboard in the front room lies the dagger ready for its final plunge home'.

Also exhibited are weapons (guns and shotguns) connected with two terrorist organisations – the Army of the Provisional Government (the

The art of the forger

Tartan Army) and the Workers' Party of Scotland. From 1971 to 1975 the Tartan Army committed various crimes, including conspiracy, bank robbery and breaking into explosive stores and military establishments to obtain arms and ammunition. To boost their funds, the Workers' Party of Scotland carried out five bank robberies in Central Scotland during 1971.

A star exhibit is a framed dyed strip of skin belonging to William Burke, who, along with William Hare, killed 16 people so that their bodies could be used by anatomists at Edinburgh University. Burke was hanged in 1829. The fragment of skin was sent anonymously to an *Evening Times* reporter in 1905.

In another section, an early 'mugshot' book is interesting, as, instead of there being separate front and profile shots of the prisoners, one photograph incorporates both. Apparently, at the time photographs were very expensive, so, instead of taking front and profile shots, by using a mirror the same effect was obtained from one photograph. Hands were also shown in the photographs because in the days of heavy industry and dock working, people suffered distinctive injuries to their hands – scarring, fingers or fingertips missing, and so on. These, plus tattoos, helped with identification.

Also on show are tipstaffs, metal-tipped staffs, or staves, that, as far back as ancient times, people in authority carried to designate their position. Gradually, they came to symbolise authority under the Crown and police officers carried them as identification before the introduction of warrant cards.

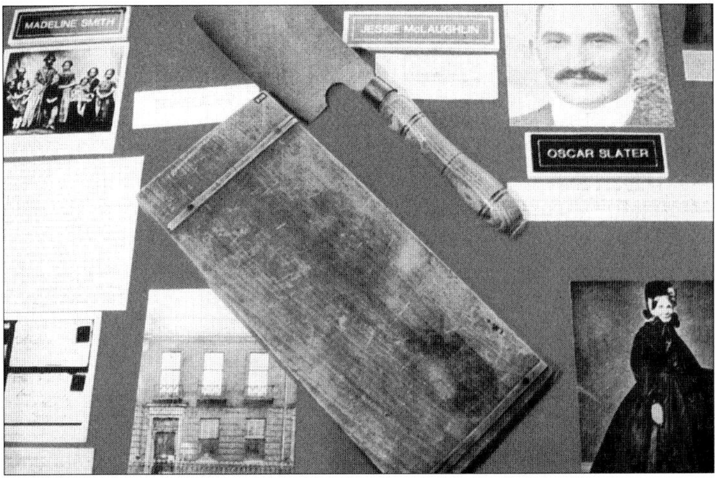

Square Mile of Murder display case showing the meat cleaver used to murder Jessie McPherson and a block of wood showing the bloody footprint that was the evidence that convicted Jessie McLachlan of the murder

Older tipstaffs were hollow, usually unscrewing at the top. The hollow staffs were intended to hold a warrant, either providing details of the holder's office or for the arrest of a named person. Scottish tipstaffs were about six inches long and generally made of wood with silver caps. Those used by Glasgow's police were often decorated with a crown. As tipstaffs were expensive to produce, warrant cards replaced them in the late 19th century. Despite the police no longer using them, the link with the past is visible in the shoulder insignia worn by senior officers in Scotland – crossed tipstaffs in a thistle-leaf wreath.

Among the forgery exhibits are documents, banknotes and printing plates. The plate engraved by hand on roofing slate showed such exceptional artistic ability that the court dealt leniently with the forger, giving him only a nine-months sentence, after which police officers thought it worthwhile to find him a job. But old habits die hard and, a few years later, he was arrested on another forgery charge.

The story is also told of Glasgow's best-known forger, photographer John Henry Greatrex, caught by Superintendent Alexander McColl, who traced him to America. How did McColl do it? Knowing that Greatrex and his girlfriend, who had fled with him, would be in need of money, he put an advertisement in the city newspapers for a Scots photographic assistant. The girlfriend applied for the job and unwittingly led McColl to Greatrex.

Four of Glasgow's most publicised murder cases of the past feature in the Square Mile of Murder section, the square mile referring to the radius of the area around Charing Cross where all the murders were committed. The four cases are those of: Madeleine Smith, alleged in 1857 to have poisoned her lover, Pierre L'Angelier, but whose case was found 'not proven' (see Chapter 19); Dr Edward William Pritchard, hanged in 1865 for poisoning his wife and mother-in-law and the last person to be publicly executed in Glasgow; Oscar Slater, wrongly convicted in 1909 of murdering 83-year-old Miss Marion Gilchrist and eventually released after 19 years in prison; and Jessie McLachlan, convicted of murdering servant Jessie McPherson with a meat cleaver. Jessie McLachlan was sentenced to hang in 1862, but this was commuted to penal servitude for life. She had been trapped by a clever doctor who got her to leave her bloody footprint on a block of wood. When the print was compared with the bloody footprint found on the floor of Jessie McPherson's bedroom, the doctor said that they corresponded 'with a degree of accuracy which was quite marvellous'. The wooden block with the footprint is displayed here, as is the meat cleaver.

The drugs showcase has illegal drugs, syringes, weighing equipment, and items such as opium and cannabis pipes. Among the drugs are LSD tabs that dealers target at youngsters. When the tabs, tiny squares soaked in the drug, are placed on the tongue, the drug is absorbed into the system. To attract children, some have pictures of cuddly toys. There is also a block of black cannabis taken from a house where it was hidden inside a small wall security box.

A model of a Second World War officer wearing a blue-painted steel helmet and carrying a gas mask is displayed in the War Cabinet. Of the same vintage is an experimental white helmet with POLICE on the front and STOP on the back. It also has a blue flashing light, the idea being that officers could wear it to direct traffic in the blackout. Fortunately, it never got beyond the experimental stage, as any officer wearing it would have been a target for ridicule. Among the war exhibits is one of the only two references to policewomen in the museum, a 1940s' uniform. The other reference is a dressed model of a year 2000 Strathclyde policewoman.

When Emily Miller, the first policewoman, joined the force in 1915, she was on her own for four years until another ten women were recruited. Earlier, various women's organisations had urged that female detectives be engaged, especially to interview female witnesses. In December 1911, however, a meeting of the Magistrates' Committee declined to entertain the proposal on the grounds that 'it was, according to the law and long continued practice in Scotland, impractical, and if adopted would result in no good purpose being served'.

The Communications section ranges from rattles to radios. In the 19th century, the only means by which constables could call for help from their colleagues in the area were wooden rattles and clappers, three small pieces of wood slackly tied with string, which, when shaken up and down, made a loud noise. (It is believed that this is how the saying 'run like the clappers' originated.) By the end of the century, most forces had adopted whistles.

Glasgow's police got the telephone in 1880, when lines linked the Western and Central police stations, a distance of about two miles. Six years later, all police stations in the city were connected with the general telephone exchange.

Police (and fire) signalboxes came next. In 1891, 14 ornamental red cast-iron boxes were installed, each containing a telephone and topped by a gas lamp. By 1914, there were 56 boxes, which could be entered only by a police officer using a special key. By 1931, most of the boxes contained electric grills, 'for the use of men taking their refreshments'.

In 1932, the arrival of Percy Sillitoe brought the standard blue kiosk, the Tardis, as it became known, a miniature police station with direct telephone communication with divisional headquarters. Signal lamps on top of the boxes alerted officers when stations wished to contact them. Sillitoe believed that, with a police box on virtually every beat, officers could go straight from home to their beat, thereby 'preventing criminals from counting upon an almost certain lull in police patrols in every 24 hours when for about ten minutes at 6 pm, 2 pm and 10 pm all constables were busily making their way to or from the police station on their way on or off duty'. On arrival at their beat, officers called headquarters from the police box and reported that they had started work. By the 1960s, the use of personal radios by beat officers made the police box obsolete.

There is an exhibit of a Speakerphone, brought out in 1931 and in use until the mid 1960s. Smaller than police boxes, they were vandalproof and the public could use them free of charge to summon Fire, Police or Ambulance. Another important feature was the light on top that could be turned on to indicate to any constable in the area that a member of the public needed assistance. The Speakerphone, and the simplicity of its operation, was a godsend at the time, as few people had telephones.

A photograph of one of the 14 red cast-iron police and fire signalboxes that were introduced in 1891

Still on communications, there's a carefully posed photograph of two well-dressed plainclothes policemen sitting in Glasgow's first radio-equipped police van, introduced by Sillitoe in 1935. They had obviously dressed for the occasion, as one was wearing spats. A year later, radio (then called the wireless) was an established form of communication in the city and the police, with 29 vehicles fitted with radio equipment, boasted of a three-minute response to any call for assistance by the public. By 1937, 277 arrests were attributed to the radio system.

A popular exhibit is the birch (a bundle of dry twigs bound together) and birching board, used in Glasgow until 1948 for male offenders from the age of eight upwards, who were taken to court and sentenced to a particular number of strokes. Depending on the age of the offender, the size and the weight of the birch varied, the lightest being used for the youngest, and so on. Lawbreakers were placed face down on the board, strapped on at the arms, knees and ankles, and then given the designated number of strokes. The Isle of Man used the birch long after Glasgow and the last boy to be birched there was from Glasgow. It did have some effect, as he vowed he would never go back to the island.

On leaving this fascinating museum, most people vow to return, as there is too much to see and to take in on one visit. What is taken in, however, is the uphill battle that the police have to keep law and order and how much we owe them for fighting it.

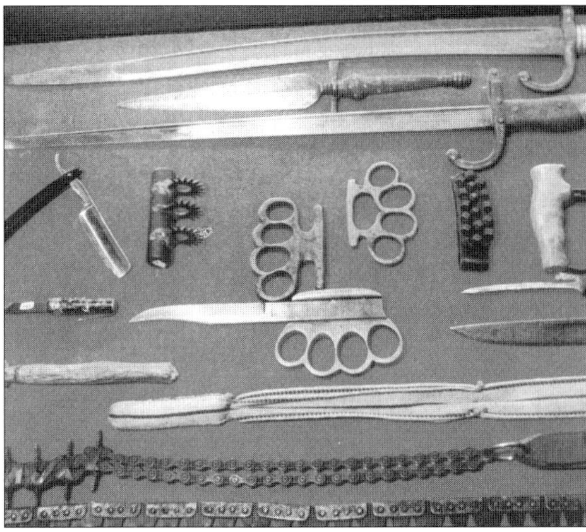

Some of the weapons taken from the Glasgow gangs that were cleared up by chief constable Sir Percy Sillitoe after he joined the Glasgow Police Force in 1932

CHAPTER 15

THE VILLAGE WITHIN THE CITY

Abbey National House, St Vincent Street

Massive though it is, nothing about the façade of 301 St Vincent Street suggests that the building operates like a 'village', with shop, restaurant, café, franchised eating facilities, bank, mortgage centre and infrastructure services. It also has extensive gardens at ground level, terraced rooftop gardens, a leisure club with squash courts, a 25-metre pool, café and bar.

Situated beside the M8 – in fact, the M8 city off-ramp runs through the car park – the colossus of tinted glass and granite is owned by Abbey National plc and is used as the headquarters of its Life Division.

The building was built for Britoil in 1983 and, with a floor area of over 500,000 square feet and 130 miles of cabling for the computer and communications services, is believed to be the largest private office development in Scotland. It took three years and 1.5 million man-hours to build, and cost £35.9 million. Ownership passed from Britoil to BP Exploration in 1987 and to Abbey National plc in June 1995, when it was named Abbey National House. Previously on the site was the Greek-style Unitarian Church, designed by architect J. T. Rochhead in 1854, which remained a place of worship until 1983, when it was demolished because of the deterioration of the structure.

With its marble floors and walls, escalators, glazed atrium and double-height mall, the interior of Abbey National House is more akin to an upmarket shopping centre than an office complex. Among the features in the mall are weeping fig trees and an astrological clock designed and built by Alan Hamshere of Gateside in Fife. Weighing over 700 lbs, it took 15 months to complete and, among other things, shows the time in 24 countries, the position of the sun and the moon in the zodiac and even the times of high tide on the Clyde. Near the clock is a reminder of the site's past – two female plaster figures from the Unitarian Church. There were originally twelve figures, from whose outstretched arms lamps were suspended. Britoil dismantled and restored the church's organ, which is now in the University of Glasgow's Bute Hall.

Those sitting in the eating areas that overlook the ground-floor gardens can easily forget that they are in the centre of Glasgow, for all they can see through the glazed curtain walling is the mature greenery that hides the neighbouring buildings.

Unique to Glasgow, and set one above the other like the decks of a liner, the landscaped roof terraces at the east and west ends of the building are lush with bushes, plants and trees, including a bonsai that was 120 years old when Britoil received it. Staff who want to take advantage of good weather by spending their lunch breaks in the sunshine can do so without leaving the building, as there are seats among the plants and grassy areas. The view from the east terraces is a close-up of the steeple of Alexander 'Greek' Thomson's masterpiece, the St Vincent Street Church.

Abbey National House participates in Glasgow's Doors Open Day scheme and a visit there is really worthwhile because, as already mentioned, it is not just another massive modern building without character. Internally, it is designed like an exclusive shopping mall and with its shop, eateries, bank, leisure centre, gardens and infrastructure, it really does operate like a 'village within the city'. In fact, all that is lacking to make it independent of the city is living accommodation.

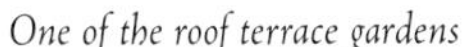
One of the roof terrace gardens

Feature astrological clock

CHAPTER 16

A HIDDEN GEM

Britannia Music Hall, Trongate

Day after day, hundreds of people walk along the Trongate towards Glasgow Cross, passing on their way a dilapidated Italianate blue-painted Victorian building with an amusement arcade on its ground floor. What they don't know is that on the second and third floors is one of Glasgow's hidden gems – what remains of the famous Britannia Music Hall, the oldest surviving theatre in Scotland and the second oldest in Britain.

The Britannia opened in 1859 and closed in 1938. It was then forgotten about for 60 years until it was discovered, remarkably well preserved, sealed behind a false ceiling. Astonishingly, the balcony and upper part of the auditorium are intact, as are the ornate plasterwork and wood panelling. The balcony, running round three sides of the theatre, still has its curving narrow fixed wooden benches. Above the stage, some wooden blocks and pulleys

The façade of the building that contains the old Britannia Music Hall

used to hang backcloths remain in place, as does the fixture for the acrobats' trapeze. What was the stalls area on the first floor has long since disappeared, devoured by the various businesses that have occupied the space since the Britannia closed.

It is possible to imagine what the theatre looked like in its heyday as there are still vestiges of gold paint on the arches and pillars, and the vaulted ceiling still has its design of gold stars on a blue background. Patches of the original blue-and-red stencilling on the walls supporting the arches can also be made out. The Britannia could seat 600 people, with standing room for another 400.

Music hall in Glasgow developed from an informal form of entertainment held in the backrooms of pubs. These events were called 'free-and-easies' and were presided over by a verbose chairman who would encourage customers to get up on a platform and sing a popular song, with everyone else joining in with the choruses. Such was the popularity of the free-and-easies that the publicans, realising that entertainment was a money-making business, began enlarging their premises so that they could pack more people in. These expanded pub halls, or concert saloons, were followed by larger purpose-built music halls, such as David Brown's Royal Music Hall in Dunlop Street, where the smoke was so dense that the stage could hardly be

The Britannia Music Hall around 1892

seen. Shearer's Whitebait Concert Rooms in St Enoch's Wynd started as a free-and-easy in 1857. Admission was 6d, with a free refreshment or cigar thrown in. The Whitebait, famous for pioneering 'girlie' shows, lost its licence in the 1870s after a public protest about the lewdness of some of the acts.

The Britannia started life in the Trongate in 1857 as Campbell's Music Saloon, an unlicensed music hall. By 1859 it was owned by John Brand and known as the Britannia. The entrance was sandwiched between shopfronts and was marked only by two gas lanterns. There was a small hallway with ticket booths on either side, and the auditorium had a single wooden balcony with bench seating throughout.

Along with its rival, the Scotia Music Hall in nearby Stockwell Street, which opened in 1863, the Britannia avoided the sale of alcohol for long periods of its existence. Brand, who managed the business between 1860 and 1869, was said to have conducted it 'along temperance lines', and subsequent police reports detailing the debauchery of other similar premises described the Britannia as a model of good management and decorum.

By the 1870s, music hall was hugely profitable, with proprietors packing people into their premises to an extent that would be frightening today. There were no safety regulations, and a newspaper described how 'the sudden withdrawal of bolts' at the Britannia brought 'the flying open of the doors and the rush of men, women and boys to get inside and secure their

Part of the balcony, which was discovered behind false ceiling

places.' H. T. Rossborough, proprietor from 1869 to 1887, when he died, was said to have amassed 'a handsome fortune from the Britannia'. Another owner, William Kean, who took over from Rossborough's widow in 1892, was not so lucky. After spending thousands of pounds on refurbishment, he was driven to bankruptcy by competition from rival establishments.

Television programmes like *The Good Old Days* give the impression that music-hall audiences good-naturedly applauded all the acts, good or bad. While they may have done so at some theatres, at the 'Brit' acts that did not find favour had rotten fruit, eggs, and even rivets, hurled at them. A regular feature at the Brit was the Friday amateur night when, much to the delight of the audience, any aspiring artiste who failed to come up to standard was yanked off the stage by the manager, using a long pole with a hook at the end.

At the end of the 1890s, Glasgow had more theatres per head of population than any other city in the country and the Britannia was the Grand Old Lady of them all. All the big names of the day appeared there, including Dan Leno, Marie Lloyd, Vesta Tilley, Little Tich and the great Sir Harry Lauder, who topped the bill in August 1897. Admission prices were: Body of Hall 3d; Pit Stalls (cushioned) 4d; Circle 6d. Doors opened at 7 pm with overture at 7.30 pm A great favourite at the Brit was Glasgow-born Marie Loftus, who came from Glasgow-Irish stock and went on to become a great star of the Victorian age as the 'Hibernian Hebe' and later the 'Sarah Bernhardt of the Halls'. Marie toured all over the Empire and, on her regular return visits to Glasgow, would play to packed houses. After one appearance at the Britannia, when there was not an inch of unoccupied room, over 1,000 people gathered outside the hall, waiting for her to appear after the performance. Irish singers who sang evocative songs of the homeland were extremely popular at the Brit, there being a strong Irish immigrant presence in the locality.

When South African showman Albert Hubner took over the management of the Britannia in 1892, he showed silent films as an added attraction. Although he renamed the building Hubner's Cinematograph, however, the music-hall side came first, and the *Glasgow Weekly Programme* said: 'To those who like music-hall business, the BEST and CHEAPEST is undoubtedly the Britannia in Trongate.'

BEST and CHEAPEST it may have been, but by the early 1900s competition from new custom-built music halls had halted the Brit's popularity, and in 1903, after Hubner left to run the Alexandra Music Hall in Cowcaddens, it closed.

The Britannia remained closed until extrovert Yorkshire-born showman Albert Ernest Pickard, who owned the adjacent waxworks, leased it in 1906. Pickard renamed his whole complex the Panopticon, 'a place where you can see everything', he said. According to the following report from the *Daily Record and Mail* he was right: 'Apart from the variety of entertainment, people will find plenty of attractions in the building. There are various tableaux in wax, these including a representation of a torture chamber of the Middle Ages, the Story of a Paris crime and human sacrifices in Dahomey. In addition, there are various mechanical and automatic machines and electric rifle shooting machines and many paintings and statues.' There were also freak shows and an American museum on the top floor. An example of Pickard's zany sense of humour was the large sign outside the Panopticon, reading MIND THE STEP. There was no step. It was just his idea of fun, his maxim, which he was always quoting, being, 'You've got to 'ave a bit o' fun, you know, life's all fun.'

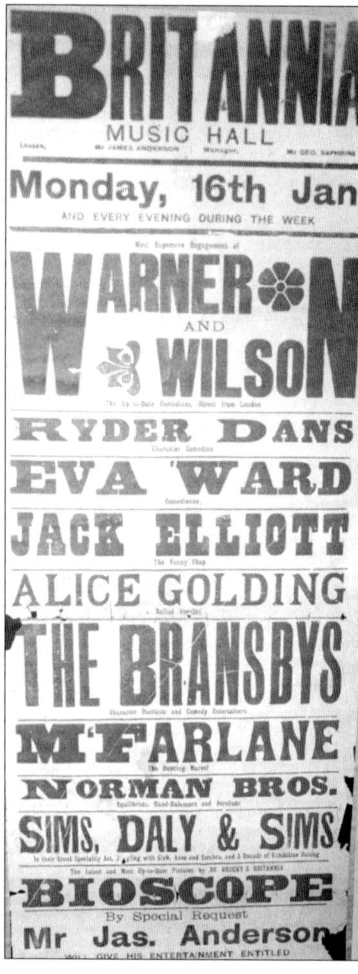

Britannia playbill

Although the Panopticon, or Britannia Theatre of Varieties and Panopticon, to give it its full name, was doing well, in 1908 Pickard opened a zoo in the theatre's basement. He had decided to compete with a most influential showman in Glasgow, E. H. Bostock, who ran the Scottish Zoo in New City Road. To publicise his new venture – Pickard's Noah's Ark – he drove a lorry decorated to represent Noah's Ark around the city.

As it cost only 2d to get into Noah's Ark, against 6d to get into the Scottish Zoo, and the Trongate was in the centre of town while New City Road was slightly out of town, Bostock naturally worried about the competition. A battle between Bostock and Pickard then began. Bostock objected to Pickard's title, saying that the Wombell Menagerie had been using it before Pickard was even heard of. The two men then started a tit-for-tat advertising campaign. In one advertisement Pickard printed the slogan, 'Truth is a rock upon which all may stand.' Bostock retaliated by stating 'MONKEYS AND PARROTS DO NOT CONSTITUTE A ZOO.' The battle might have gone on forever except that the New City Zoo was not doing well and, a year later, all the animals were sold. Bostock changed the place into a gigantic roller-skating rink, leaving Pickard free to advertise his Noah's Ark as the only zoo in Glasgow.

At the Panopticon, performers were often amateurs, and Pickard always declared proudly that he was partly responsible for the fame of Laurel and Hardy, as the 16-year-old Stan Jefferson, later Stan Laurel, made his first stage appearance at the Panopticon.

Stan's ambition was to be a comedian, although his father, Arthur Jefferson, manager of the Metropole Theatre in Stockwell Street, wanted him to go into theatre management. To get his ambition off the ground, Stan asked Pickard if he would give him a 'try-on' to see what he could do. When Pickard asked why he should, Stan answered, 'I'm funny.'

Pickard agreed, and Stan went on stage with jokes and comedy routines he had put together by watching acts at the Metropole. He had even paid a half-crown to a Glasgow musician for an original song.

Meanwhile, Stan's father was passing the Panopticon when the doorman said, 'Young Stan's doing well.' 'Doing what well?' Stan's father asked. 'He's on stage,' said the doorman. Stan's father went into the building and, in company with Pickard, watched Stan's performance. When Stan saw his father, his first inclination was to flee the stage. He didn't, however, and went on to finish his act, which was greeted with a good round of applause.

When Stan went backstage, he was on a high. His head was full of the applause he had just received, and it was not until he was taking his make-up off that it hit him that he would have to face his father. Getting out of his costume, he rushed out of the theatre and jumped on a tram home. As it passed the Metropole, however, he decided to get off and face his father there and then and get it over with. When he did, he got a surprise. Instead of being angry, his father said, 'Well, congratulations. Sit down. Want a whisky and soda?' With that, Stan gaped at his father and then, to use his own words, 'I made a proper fool of myself. I burst into tears.' After asking where Stan's material had come from, his father asked where he had found the magnificent checked trousers he had worn. When Stan told his father that they were cut down from his finest double-checked trousers that he wore to race meetings, he took the news surprisingly well. Later Stan admitted that his act was awful, 'bloody awful, in fact', he said. That the applause was warm he guessed was because the audience felt sorry for him.

There is a theory that Stan's débût didn't take part in the Britannia building but in the annexe next door, the reasoning being that the Britannia had seating and featured a resident review company appearing nightly. The room Stan later described was curtained off, with no seating. This theory is probably correct, as a section of the Panopticon was turned into a miniature music hall in which the audience stood while the ladies' orchestra that accompanied the acts had the only seats in the primitive surroundings.

In 1911, the debonair Jack Buchanan, who went on to become a Hollywood star, made his first professional stage appearance at the Panopticon. He was booked for a week, and while that might sound grand, it was like being thrown in at the deep end as the Panopticon audiences had a reputation for being the hardest to please. Jack found this to be true. His debut was a disaster, his fate being virtually sealed even before he went on because, when the notice 'Extra Turn', denoting a newcomer, went up on the side of the stage, the audience began baying for blood. Jack's appearance was greeted with catcalls and, when he started his routine, he could not be heard above the shouting and verbal abuse, the most polite being 'Get aff'. Although Jack gave it a good try, he 'dried' and left the stage. However, when a fellow performer waiting to go on, said, 'Cheer up. Wait till you see what I get when I go on, and I'm top of the bill!' he felt slightly better.

Jack finished his week there, as the management of the Panopticon regarded his reception as vastly entertaining to the audience. He later said that his debut must have been a world record in 'getting the bird' at each of his four daily appearances, or 24 times in his first week.

Pickard's Britannia Theatre had four shows daily and continued the old Britannia tradition of Friday amateur nights when the manager stood in the wings equipped with a long pole to yank off acts that failed to meet the modest standards of the establishment. Pickard had his own inimitable way of dealing with rowdy patrons. He would sit at the top of a ladder at the side of the stage, throwing screw nails at those exceeding the permitted bounds of rowdiness. Amateur night at the Panopticon was such a riot that the 2d seats cost 4d that evening.

At the beginning of the First World War, Pickard decided that the future of the entertainment business in Glasgow lay in the cinema, not in the theatre. He therefore sold his Gaiety Theatre in Clydebank and built his first cinema, the Casino, at Townhead. The Casino was a gold mine and, to build on its success, he opened the Seamore Palace in Maryhill Road. Although his cinemas took up most of his time, Pickard didn't neglect the Panopticon and in April 1915 was advertising, 'The declared ambition of the Kaiser, before being despatched to St Helena, is to visit the Panopticon.' For his waxworks he advertised a Half Lady and 999,999 other Freaks, including the Kaiser. However, an advertisement of 1916 illustrated the popularity of the pictures.

PICKARD'S SEAMORE PALACE
UNUSUAL BUSINESS

PICKARD'S TOWNHEAD CASINO
EXTRA BUSINESS

PICKARD'S PANOPTICON
ROTTEN BUSINESS

By the 1920s, Pickard's Panopticon, or the 'Pots and Pans' as it was called, had begun to slip into a decline. Pickard then turned it into a cinema, the Tron Cinema, with variety acts being put on as an added attraction to films instead of films being an added attraction to variety shows.

Glasgow man Thomas McCourt remembers visiting the Panopticon in the mid 1930s, when he was about four or five years old. Seats in the stalls cost 4d, which was a lot, as his father earned only about £2.10s a week as a carter and salesman for Barr's lemonade. Even as a child, Thomas thought the hall was quite small, but the gold paint impressed him. He also remembers there was a lot of dark blue and green in the décor. Thomas, his father, mother and three sisters sat in the stalls on one of the bare unpadded wooden benches with no backs. The stage was about five feet higher than the stalls, and between it and the benches was a small curtained-off area for the band, which consisted of a conductor, a fiddler, an accordion player and a drummer.

According to Thomas, there was a live act before the films which were projected on to a screen about 18 feet square with a black border around it. He can remember seeing black-and-white cartoons – *The Three Little Pigs* and *Felix the Cat* – and a film, *The Three Stooges*.

Thomas was also in the theatre once when there was a 'Sods' Opera', as he said the amateur performances were called. Apparently, the acts were awful that day and there were shouts of 'Get them aff', accompanied by a barrage of vegetables directed towards the stage. As the theatre was close to the fruit market in Bell Street, there was no shortage of rotten tomatoes, etc. Some boys liked to half-peel the tomatoes so that they would hit the amateur with a splat. Another favourite trick was to chuck fresh horse dung smuggled into the theatre in a paper bag.

It was only two or three years after Thomas McCourt's visits to the Panopticon that it closed down. Pickard's son Peter had taken over the management in 1931, and by 1938, the premises were listed in Glasgow's City Valuation Roll as empty. Although the theatre had survived for 81 years under various names – Campbell's Music Saloon, the Britannia, Hubner's Cinematograph, the Britannia Theatre of Varieties and Panopticon, the Tron Cinema and, in 1927, back to the Panopticon – to the people of Glasgow it was always familiarly known as the Brit.

As already mentioned, the Brit lay empty and undisturbed for over 60 years. A couple of books on architecture made a brief mention that it existed, but nothing was done about it until the archaeologist and historian Judith Bowers was shown around the old building in the Trongate with the amusement arcade on the ground floor. When she climbed the staircase to the second floor, she couldn't believe what she saw – a theatre. To use her words, 'It was magical, like walking into a wonderland.' (Pickard had sold the building to a tailor in 1938, after which the false ceiling hiding the theatre was put in.)

Judith was so excited by what she saw that she set up the Britannia Panopticon Music Hall Trust, which hopes to raise funds, firstly, to rescue the building, and secondly, to restore the theatre and possibly turn it into a museum of theatre and film, combined with exhibition space.

When those involved with the Trust started searching the spaces between the floor and the false ceiling, they found dozens of cigarette packets, matchboxes and old coins, one a half-crown, which must have been a fortune to the working class crowds who frequented the theatre. There were also pipes, buttons, jewellery, newspapers, posters advertising forthcoming attractions and even a Cadbury's sweetie. That the building still stood was a wonder, as thousands of matches had been dropped, many unused. At least 1,000 objects were found, which were displayed at the People's Palace from 24 June to 27 September 1999.

Members of the cast of *High Road* who went to have a look at the theatre were captivated by it. They found it hard to believe that they were standing in a theatre where Harry Lauder and Stan Laurel had performed.

Let's hope that the money can be found to preserve the old Brit. It's very special as it is the second oldest theatre in Britain, and the oldest music hall. As the building is the subject of a Council repair notice however, and the roof needs to be replaced, something needs to be done quickly to ensure that this 'hidden gem' doesn't vanish.

Just some of the hundreds of matchboxes found beneath the floor of the theatre

CHAPTER 17

THE MOST EXQUISITE INTERIOR IN THE WEST END

22 Park Circus

Nothing in the classical facade of 22 Park Circus indicates that it is any different from its neighbours, certainly not that it hides the most exquisite interiors in the area, if not in the city, its only rival being the City Chambers. In fact, the only people who seem to be aware of the splendour of the interior are those with weddings on their mind, since Glasgow City Council turned the building into the most magnificent set of marriage rooms in the country.

The first wedding ceremony took place on 13 April 1994, and since then couples from all over the world have queued up to tie the knot in the grandeur of 22 Park Circus. Each of the five marriage rooms has its own distinctive character, and all are decorated and furnished to the highest standard. As the building is listed both inside and outside, nothing can be changed, even to the extent that, when the Council wanted to put small

Façade of 22 Park Circus

plaques on the doors to say which room was which, it had to get permission from Historic Scotland.

Park Circus was built in the 1860s, and as all the houses in the area were sold as empty shells, the purchasers had to commission architects to design them internally. Therefore, when industrialist Walter Macfarlane, who owned the Saracen Foundry, bought No. 22, he commissioned architect James Boucher, who had worked for him before, to design its interior. Macfarlane made a wise choice, as Boucher gave the house the most exotic opulent interior in the city. (The City Chambers were still to be built.)

The house was complete by 1874 and, to complement the richness of the Italian Renaissance-style décor, Macfarlane began filling it with works of art and fine furniture. (An inventory taken after his death in 1885 detailed the contents and the layout of the house's four floors – lower ground: the servants' quarters and utility areas; ground floor: the library, dining room, morning room, billiard room, Turkish bath and conservatory; first floor: the drawing room and master bedroom; second floor: guest bedrooms.)

After Walter Macfarlane's death, his widow lived in the house until Walter Macfarlane Junior took possession in 1888. As the Macfarlanes were childless, they had adopted a nephew of Walter's with the same name, and when he and his wife took over the house, thinking the décor old-fashioned, they commissioned Glasgow architect James Salmon Junior to refurbish it in the new Glasgow Style.

The magnificent Italian Renaissance-style arcaded hall

Although refurbishment mainly took the form of relining the walls of the main public rooms with wooden panelling and adding wooden overmantels to the fireplaces, some structural changes were made, such as dividing the conservatory to make an Art Nouveau smoking room. As most of the new woodwork was the work of Francis Derwent Wood, the modelling master at the Glasgow School of Art, without interfering with Boucher's lavish Italianate interior, the alterations added some of the finest Glasgow Style to the house, giving it the best of two eras.

The house remained in the Macfarlane family until 1934, when the managing director of an Italian bank bought it. It then became known as the Casa d'Italia, 'the Italian House' and, after serving for a time as the Italian consulate, it was used by Glasgow's Italian community as a social club until 1990, when the building was put up for sale. Fortunately, during its sojourn as the Casa d'Italia, the owner's funds were limited, saving the interior from alteration, unlike its neighbours, which have mostly been converted into offices. The new owner of the house, together with Historic Scotland, set about restoring Boucher's magnificent Italianate decoration.

The splendour of the Italian Renaissance-style arcaded hall is stunning. Supported by Ionic columns, the domed ceiling is divided into sections by superb plasterwork archways representing Vice and Virtues; Four Arts – Acting, Painting, Singing and Sculpting; Four Ages of Man and Four Continents – Europe, America, Africa and Asia. The décor is green, terra-cotta and gold, with columns in imitation sienna marble.

On the left of the hall is the Lomond Marriage Room, panelled in dark wood and once Walter Macfarlane's library. His initials are incorporated into the intricate plasterwork on each of the four corners of the ceiling and, as people then mostly chose their plasterwork designs from samples in catalogues, the birds, garlands and flowers ornamenting the cornice and frieze are unique to the house. The original fireplace, heavily carved in Jacobean style, was partly covered with a wood surround in the 'modernisation' of the late 1890s.

Behind the library is the Lomond waiting room, originally the morning room, where Mrs Macfarlane would have entertained her daytime callers. The colour scheme is similar to that of the library, but lighter. It is not, however, only the colouring that makes the room more feminine – the décor is in 'Louis Revival' style, with a white marble fireplace, heavy gilding and intricate plasterwork. The frieze features cherubs, swags and flowers, and the cornice incorporates plaster faces of British writers and poets such as Robert Burns, William Shakespeare and Sir Walter Scott. As the original furnishings included a broadwood piano, it is probable the room was used as a 'family room', as it was smaller and less grand than the drawing room.

Across the hall is the Kelvin Marriage Room, originally the dining room, as indicated by the carvings above the door of fish, poultry, fruit and a wine glass. Like the library, it has dark wood panelling, complemented by a colour scheme of dark green, beige, red and, on the breathtaking cornicework, several shades of gold. The magnificent black marble fireplace has tiled sides and a wooden overmantel with carving thought to depict the French poet La Fontaine's fable 'The Stork and the Fox'. Originally, the room held a mahogany table around which were 20 chairs upholstered in crimson velvet.

To the rear of the hall is the divided conservatory, which is now a favourite place to have wedding photographs taken. The delicate embossed metal end walls, lacy arcade and roof with a scalloped pattern of glazing bars were the work of the Saracen Foundry. When Walter Macfarlane Junior had

The Kelvin Marriage Room originally the dining room of the house

the conservatory divided to make a smoking room, a feature was made of the partitioning wall. Stained-glass panels depicting the five 'senses' (sight, touch, taste, smell and hearing) were set into an alcove topped by colourful tiling representing Scotland, England and Ireland, Wales being left out because it is not a kingdom, but a principality.

Through from the conservatory is what was the male domain of the Macfarlane household – the Turkish bathroom, heating and cooling rooms and billiard room, all interconnecting. What was once the Turkish bathroom is now the Registrar's Room, with arches, a fabulous golden-glazed dome and a fireplace with Moorish tiles. Among the carvings decorating the panelling are ghoulish faces described as being of the 'Spook School'. By law, there has to be a room available for those wanting to pay only the statutory marriage fee, and the small but exotic Registrar's Room is the ideal venue, as only four people can attend such weddings.

One of the stained-glass panels in the conservatory

The former billiard room, now the Avon Room, has dark woodwork, a black marble fireplace and a splendid dome with scalloped ironwork set with hand-painted glass in shades of yellow, pink, blue and green. It also has a remarkable tiled and painted frieze portraying male pursuits that are split into four categories: Health, Strength, Courage and Fortitude.

The carvings on the fireplace show an old man and a young man and, although it looks out of place in a wedding room, the built-in banquette beside the fireplace cannot be removed, as nothing in the building can be altered. It does however, provide an unusual setting for the all-important wedding photographs and, remembering the original function of the room, it is easy to picture Victorian and Edwardian gentlemen lolling on it, cues in hand, awaiting their turn to play billiards.

Like everything else in the building, the staircase is magnificent, the décor and features matching those of the hall. It has a stained-glass window and on the quarter-landings are round marble wall plaques signed by H. Gerhardt Roma (1874). One plaque shows Venus, the other Cupid.

The first floor is astonishing – a magnificent upper hall with Corinthian columns, archways, spectacular plasterwork, a gallery with gilded cast-iron balustrade and a scalloped and glazed dome similar to that in the billiard room but even more staggering. Surrounded by such opulence, it is hard to believe the building was once a private dwelling.

Outside the drawing room, now the Katrine Wedding Room seating 55 guests, there's a gold-leaf plaque on the ceiling with the date 1874 – the year the house was completed – incorporated into the design.

Just as carvings above the dining-room door indicated the function of the room, those above the drawing-room door, of cherubs playing musical instruments, show it was used for entertainment. Reflecting the importance that music and entertainment played in the use of the room, the magnificent wooden overmantel is decorated with two carved musicians. The room has an elaborate and unusual ceiling cornice featuring flowers, foliage, birds, squirrels and toadstools.

A bird's-eye view of the upper hall's gilded arches and amazing scalloped cupola

Mrs Macfarlane must have had a hand in decorating what was the master bedroom, now the Clyde Suite. It's light and feminine, with a white marble fireplace and a flowery wallpaper frieze. Above the fireplace is an overmantel incorporating a lantern display cabinet with leaded glass decorated with a typical Art Nouveau rose design in the shape of an ogee (a double curve bending first one way and then the other).

The first thing to do on reaching the second-floor gallery is to look over the gilded balustrade to get a sweeping view of the magnificent upper hall. From the gallery, there's a bird's-eye view of the amazing scalloped cupola bordered with red, yellow and white glass in a stylised flower design. There's also a close-up of the Corinthian columns and the gilded arches supporting the cupola. Each main arch carries a plaster cast of a face flanked on each side by a date. No one is sure what the dates relate to, but the faces are of Carlyle, Gladstone, Ruskin and, it is thought, Macfarlane. If the suggestion that the dates refer to when the men were born is right, however, the face thought to be Macfarlane's could not be his, as he was born in 1817, not 1803, the date shown. As well as the faces and dates, scrutiny of the dense gold ornamentation reveals the words 'Wisdom, Truth, Justice and Power', thought to be Walter Macfarlane's creed.

Originally the second floor consisted of guest bedrooms in different styles and colours – a pink bedroom, a walnut bedroom, an oak bedroom, and so on. However, one little room held all the furniture Macfarlane owned when he first started in business – a pine table, a couple of chairs and a chest of drawers – and, when giving a dinner party for friends, he would take them to the room and, throwing open the door, would say, 'There, gentleman, that is how I started out in the world, and you see downstairs what I have risen to. All is due to industry, perseverance, temperance and economy. Go you and do likewise.'

As the façade gives no hint of the grandeur inside, people tend to leave the building with a feeling of 'I can't believe what I've seen'. They are impressed, however, that, for all its opulence, the décor clearly reflected the Macfarlane family's love of literature, art and music.

By the way, if you want to trace your family tree, 22 Park Circus is the place to visit. For a daily fee you can trawl your way through old parish registers, census records and registrar's records, all of which are in microfiche format for easy access.

CHAPTER 18

A TWO-FACED CLOCK

Finlay House, West Nile Street

In the foyer of the offices of James Finlay Limited (Glasgow's oldest surviving company) stands a hidden treasure, a two-faced clock, the only one of its kind in existence. One face shows Greenwich Mean Time and the other Calcutta time, reflecting the company's long trading association with India.

The history behind the clock is the study of time and motion, thought to be an expertise that developed in recent times. Nothing could be farther from the truth. To demonstrate this, let's go back to the village of Catrine in Ayrshire at the end of the 18th century.

Around 1786, Claude Alexander, who had bought Ballochmyle Estate with the fortune he had made in India, and the Glasgow merchant David Dale erected a cotton-spinning mill at Catrine, using water from the River Ayr to power the mill wheels. This source of energy worked well when there was an adequate water supply but, if there was not, production came to a standstill. This is when time and motion and two-faced clocks made their appearance.

The pine-cased two-faced clock, the only one of its kind in existence, which stands in the foyer of Finlay House in West Nile Street

William Whitelaw of Mauchline (later succeeded by apprentice R. Ferguson) was instructed to make grandfather clocks with two faces built in one casing, each face to be controlled by completely separate mechanical systems – one to be driven by normal clockwork to record local time and one to be geared to the water going over the power wheels. Consequently, if production ceased because of lack of water, the hands on the second face would stop. The difference in time recorded by the two faces showed managers and workers alike the extra hours required to be worked to bring output up to target.

From about 1790 on, these timepieces were installed in the main departments of the two spinning mills where they operated for more than 100 years. It was said that the workers, recognising their interest in maintaining production and viability, and also out of loyalty to the company, made good the lost production without extra remuneration.

In 1801, Kirkman Finlay, son of the founder of James Finlay Limited (established 1750), bought the Catrine mills and appointed as partner and manager his cousin Archibald Buchanan, whose inventive genius was responsible for the installation of two great water wheels to produce increased power from the River Ayr. Built in 1827 by Fairbairn & Lillie of Manchester and housed in a great stone mansion of their own from which resounded noise like 'thunder everlasting', they provided 200 horsepower and were the largest double iron wheels in the world.

When the mills closed in 1972, discussions took place as to what should be done with the one remaining pine-cased clock made by Ferguson in 1830, both faces of which were embellished with paintings of the two mills at Catrine and scenes depicting 'Peace and Plenty'. There were thoughts of donating it to a museum, but in the end it was decided it should reside in Glasgow at the head office of James Finlay. From 1974 to 1977, however, while Finlay House was being rebuilt, the clock was loaned to the People's Palace Museum on Glasgow Green where it proved to be a most popular exhibit. Today it's back in its rightful place in the foyer of Finlay House in West Nile Street.

Finlay's boardroom holds another treasure from the company's past, an oil painting of the great Catrine wheels, now dismantled. It was painted by a member of one of the old Catrine families, James Andrew Davidson, who worked at the mill until he moved to Beith in 1885.

CHAPTER 19

THE SECRET OF THE GRAVE

Lair No. 5, Ramshorn Churchyard

Although lair No. 5 in the New Burying Ground of the Ramshorn churchyard has a wall stone marked FLEMING, it's where Pierre Emile L'Angelier, the victim of the murder case that scandalised Britain in 1857, is buried. His lover, Madeleine Smith, was accused of poisoning him with arsenic. At the time of Pierre's death, lair No. 5, owned by James Fleming, was empty, and as Fleming's grandson, James Fleming Kennedy, and L'Angelier worked together and were friends, the family arranged for Pierre to be buried there. Although his name is not on the stone there is an entry in the record of burials stating:

> Pierre Emile L'Angelier, clerk, sudden death. Lair holder James Fleming, 5EM

Gravestone of the Fleming family, which marks the spot where Pierre Emile L'Angelier is buried

Briefly, the story of Madeleine and Pierre goes like this. Madeleine was the daughter of a successful Glasgow architect, James Smith, designer of the McLellan Galleries. L'Angelier, who was from the Channel Islands, was a penniless clerk who earned 10s a week working for a Glasgow seed firm. Pierre had pursued Madeleine after a friend had introduced him to her in Sauchiehall Street in March 1855. Because Madeleine's family disapproved of him as a suitor, however, she and Pierre had to be content with meeting secretly and writing passionate letters to each other. They first became lovers in the garden of her father's house in Rhu, where the Smith family spent their holidays.

Although the relationship between Madeleine and Pierre continued for a couple of years, she had no intention of marrying him, and when eligible suitor Billy Minnoch came along, she tried to finish with Pierre. He, however, was unwilling to let Madeleine go and threatened to show her letters to her father. Afraid of the consequences, Madeleine continued to meet him and often smuggled him into her home at 7 Blythswood Square without anyone knowing.

As Madeleine and her sister Janet shared a basement bedroom, Madeleine would wait until Janet was asleep and then either speak to Pierre through the window or let him into the house, warning him not to make a noise. Apparently Madeleine had taken a fancy to cocoa and, as her bedroom was near the kitchen, she sometimes made a cup for Pierre, especially on cold nights. When Pierre began to suffer dizziness and violent stomach pains and vomited bile, he mentioned to his landlady that a cup of chocolate had made

Pierre Emile L'Angelier

him feel ill. He didn't say he had seen Madeleine or from where he had got the chocolate. His illness lasted from February until March, when he died. He never knew that Madeleine was leading a double life and that she and Billy Minnoch were engaged and that their wedding was arranged for 18 June.

As doctors believed Pierre had been poisoned, his body was taken to the Ramshorn crypt and held there until a post-mortem examination could be carried out. In the record of the trial, Dr Hugh Thomson stated,

> 'On 31 March 1857, I received instructions from the Procurator Fiscal to attend the Ramshorn Church by order of the Sheriff to make an inspection of L'Angelier's body. Dr Steven, Dr Corbet and Dr Penny were there. The coffin was in a vault and was opened in our presence and the body taken out. I recognised it as L'Angelier's body.'

When the post-mortem was carried out the doctors were proved to be right. In fact, enough arsenic was found in his body to kill 40 men. By this time Madeleine's very frank letters to Pierre had been discovered and, when it came to light that she had been buying arsenic (for her complexion, according to her), she was arrested and charged with murder.

Madeleine's trial was held in Edinburgh, because feelings about the case were so strong in Glasgow. The rich favoured her, saying that if she had done it, it was no more than the blackmailing seducer deserved. The not-so-rich believed it was a case of a rich girl getting rid of a poor lover to marry a rich man.

When Madeleine's letters became public, they shocked the country. After all, the Victorians were so respectable that they considered even table legs to be offensive and concealed them with cloths. For a young unmarried woman to be so outspoken about sex was scandalous. Nevertheless, despite all the evidence against her, Madeleine walked free on a 'not proven' verdict. The trial, however, ruined the family socially. They left Glasgow to live in Bridge of Allan and then moved to Polmont. Mr Smith continued his practice, but half-heartedly. Mrs Smith took to her bed, and Madeleine's younger sisters never married. Madeleine did, twice.

At the age of 80, Madeleine Smith emigrated to America. She died there in 1928, aged 92.

To find lair No. 5 in the Ramshorn New Burying Ground, enter the graveyard via the gate to the right of the church and walk on until you come to a grave on the left, surrounded by a cage of tall spiked railings. The Fleming grave is the one before it.

CHAPTER 20

THE HIDDEN TRIO

Morrison's Court, Sloan's Restaurant, Argyll Arcade

The hidden trio – Morrison's Court, Sloan's Restaurant and the Argyll Arcade – can be found within a small square between Argyle Street and Buchanan Street. The history of each is interwoven, and as Morrison's Court came first we shall start with it.

MORRISON'S COURT

Morrison's Court is the oldest part of Argyle Street, and as it is entered through a pend at No. 108, it is virtually hidden to the passer-by, which is probably why most people are unaware of its existence.

Its story began in 1797, when, on a piece of vacant ground in Argyle Street, builder John Morrison built for himself a townhouse and courtyard,

Drawing of Morrison's Court showing turnpike stair

which went by the name of Morrison's Court. Included in the enclosure was a coffee/eating house, which evolved into Sloan's Restaurant, the second of our trio.

When Morrison built his courtyard, he was looked upon as being a fool who would be ruined for daring to build at what was then the extreme western limit of the city. He proved everyone wrong, nevertheless, by making his fortune and becoming a Bailie of Glasgow and a Justice of the Peace for the Under Ward of Lanarkshire. A life-size portrait of John Morrison hangs in the boardroom of Glasgow's Royal Infirmary. The inscription on the frame reads:

John Morrison of Craigends, Millerston,
of Morrison and Burns, Builders of the Royal Infirmary 1792,
Bailie of Crafts Rank 1799, Deacon Convener 1801–1802.

(Incidentally, originally it was Morison's Court, with one 'r', not two. This was the correct spelling of the name, as can be seen on the inscription on John Morison's burial stone in the Ramshorn Churchyard. The second 'r' probably crept in through carelessness, as has been the case with many other old names.)

The coffee house became a fashionable meeting place for the wealthy merchants who had built their residences around the newly formed Buchanan Street. The courtyard was the scene of many famous cockfighting contests, a favourite sport of the day, and it was not unusual for wagers as high as 1,000 guineas to be placed on one particular fight. Twice a week the stage-coach left Morrison's Court for Edinburgh, a journey of five hours. For a fare of 9s, each passenger was allowed to carry one canvas travelling bag.

Later, there were other coffee houses in the court, as Post Office Directories of the 1850s listed Laming's Coffee House, Picken's Coffee House and the Thistle Coffee House.

Architecturally, the most important feature of Morrison's Court is a turnpike stair (the best in the city), which stands on its eastern side. There is another turnpike stair on the western side but, as it has been encased in walls at a later date, it is undetectable.

John Morrison would not recognise his old court as, when Miss Catherine Cranston's husband-to-be, Major John Cochrane, gave her the building as a wedding present, she had David Barclay remodel it into the Crown Lunch and Tea Rooms. Barclay gave the building huge projecting eaves, broken by curvilinear gables, the western one bargeboarded with a pretty oriel window. George Walton was entrusted with the interior, with Charles Rennie Mackintosh providing the furnishings, including the installation of the bull's-eye panes in the staircase's lower windows, and the heavy twisted stanchions outside these windows. Of Mackintosh's basement Dutch Kitchen of 1906 nothing remains. Carved into the stone above the door leading to the east turnpike stair are two intertwined Cs standing for Catherine Cranston.

Compared with its early days, the courtyard is now an oasis of calm, as there are no stagecoaches clattering in and out over the cobblestones and no cockfights taking place.

SLOAN'S, GLASGOW'S OLDEST RESTAURANT

Hidden among the jewellers' shops in the Argyll Arcade is Sloan's, Glasgow's oldest restaurant. To reach it, enter the arcade via the Argyle Street entrance, walk 50 yards, turn left and there stands Sloan's, which, as already mentioned, can trace its origins as far back as 1797, when it started life as a coffee house in Morrison's Court.

When the Argyll Arcade was built in 1828, the coffee house was

The outside of Sloan's Restaurant from Morrison's Court

pushed through into it, providing access from two entrances – Morrison's Court and the arcade. The establishment became known as the Arcade Café and, as Glasgow developed, so did the café, which played an important part in the city's social scene.

When Queen Victoria died in 1901, Edward VII ascended the throne. A new exciting era had begun – it was time for change and the Arcade Café was not to be left behind. In 1906, David Sloan, one-time manager of Glasgow's famous Horseshoe Bar in Drury Street, bought the café. Immediately renaming it 'Sloan's Arcade Café', he put in hand extensive remodelling, in keeping with the opulence of the time. The old ground floor became a lounge bar, and several new dining rooms, a cocktail bar, aquarium and smoking room with 'cigar and tobacco divans' were formed on the first floor. However, the *pièce de résistance* was a magnificent ballroom/banqueting hall created on the second floor. With its vaulted plastered ceiling, marble fireplace and stained-glass windows, it undoubtedly was worthy of its name.

According to old menus, cock-a leekie soup was 1d and brown trout 2d. Sheep's heid was 4d, and Sloan's was the only restaurant in Glasgow to serve this delicacy every Wednesday (market day). Fortunately, or unfortunately, depending on how you view it, it does not feature on today's menu.

Although the colourful ceramic tiled entrance, grand mahogany staircase, rich old woodwork, rare acid-etched glass and ceilings heavily decorated with plaster mouldings remain, today Sloan's is a shadow of its

Above. What was the first-floor dining room, showing fine acid-etched glass and cherubs decorating the elaborate plaster frieze

Left. The grand mahogany staircase and stained-glass windows that date back to 1828

former self. The bar/dining room on the ground floor is open every day, but the first-floor dining room, which used to have a light airy café atmosphere and blackboard menu reminiscent of bygone days, is now used only for private functions, as is the former ballroom/banqueting room on the second floor.

What has been improved is the appearance of the Morrison's Court side of the building. A coat of white paint and an old-fashioned hanging sign make it look like a pleasing old inn. It is a pity that the interior does not live up to it, especially as it was once one of the finest examples of a Victorian eating house in Scotland.

ARGYLL ARCADE

The third in the historic trio is the Argyll Arcade, an off-street marvel that, although well known to Glaswegians, is a hidden delight to visitors. It is the earliest shopping centre, or mall, in Scotland and the largest specialist jewellery outlet in Britain, if not Europe. The difference in the spelling of the Argyll Arcade and Argyle Street is that in those days people spelled names any way they chose and there are as many Argyles as Argylls on maps of the

Photograph of the arcade showing the hammer-beam roof with iron tie bars, which was unique among arcades when it was built in 1828

times. Today, Argyll is accepted as correct.

The arcade was the brainchild of Glasgow mahogany exporter John Reid, whose premises were in Morrison's Court. In 1827, a fire gutted his establishment and, after the ground was cleared, not wishing to stockpile large amounts of timber again, he wondered how he could use the site to its greatest advantage. What he came up with was a covered walkway, shop-lined, with buildings of a restricted height that would link Argyle Street with Buchanan Street. There being no such construction to guide him in Scotland, he visited London in search of a prototype. Finding nothing inspiring, he went to Europe, where he studied the latest ideas in shopping habits, particularly arcades.

Having decided what he wanted, Reid asked architect John Baird to build a covered arcade to provide shops for the local gentry who lived nearby in what was then the west end of the city. Two buildings belonging to the Reid family were to be used as entrances to the arcade – a tenement in Argyle Street and one of Buchanan Street's original mansions. The final L-shape of the arcade was conditioned by a place already built on the west side of Morrison's Court. John Baird's use of a hammer-beam roof with iron tie bars was unique among arcades.

The building that originally fronted the arcade at its Buchanan Street end. The house belonged to John Reid, the originator of the arcade, and the arcade's entrance was driven through the house's front door. The Reid family lived in the top part of the house

Shortly before the Argyll Arcade's opening in July 1828, the following appeared in *The Glasgow Herald*:

> We are happy in having it in our power to announce the near completion of this beautiful interesting place of business. Every attention appears to have been paid to the comfort and luxury of those possessing the premises, and also of those who visit them in order to transaction the daily business of life. . . .
>
> 'The idea of the thoroughfare appears to have been taken from the many passages of a similar description in Paris, other cities on the continent and the Burlington Arcade in London; but for simplicity of style, elegance and lightness, we believe the Argyll Arcade exceeds any that have yet been completed. The Burlington is larger but two or three feet narrower and the roof is more enclosed there being only about one-fifth of the whole glass; whereas the Glasgow Arcade is almost entirely one sheet of latticed glass-work and the ventilation very complete; so much so, that from its construction it forms the coolest shade in summer and will be comfortably sheltered in winter. . . .

When the arcade was built, it was a highly speculative, adventurous gamble, Buchanan Street being still very much a country road leading to Port Dundas. Reid's business colleagues thought he was insane to contemplate such a venture on the outskirts of the city. As it turned out, they were wrong. The arcade quickly became a centre for quality goods and was mainly responsible for the rapid expansion of Buchanan Street as it diverted a large proportion of passenger traffic from busy Argyle Street into the calm retreat of the newer street.

The shops were obviously intended for patronage by the gentry, as, among the goods they sold were guns, jewellery, silver, musical instruments, flowers, wigs, glass, pottery and wine. It was even possible to have an 'Exact Profile Likeness' drawn by artists from London. The likeness could be in colour on ivory or paper, and, with a neat frame and glass included, the cost was one shilling.

From the start, children adored visiting the arcade, loving the sheer magic of what appeared to them to be a brightly lit cave and the excitement of entering from one street and coming out in another.

John Reid wanted to bring culture as well as trade to Glasgow, and his arcade included at the Argyle Street end a small public hall used for exhibiting paintings by contemporary artists. The West of Scotland Exhibition of Fine Arts was held there in 1829. Some of the most fashionable and famous entertainers used the hall as a small theatre. Magicians were immensely popular in Glasgow and many appeared in this venue, including Signor Blitz, one of the most refined, skilful and successful exponents of the Black Art of his day. Later, the hall was altered for business purposes.

Not long after the arcade opened a frightening incident took place. Because of the arcade's smooth pavements, a novelty at the time, cavalry officers quartered in Eglinton Street Barracks wagered that it would be impossible for a horse to keep its feet on such a surface. A young officer took up the challenge, declaring that he would ride his horse safely through the arcade at midday in full military gear, including carbine, sword and lance. This he did, charging through at Buchanan Street and emerging at Argyle Street to the utter astonishment of the shopkeepers and the terror of the public. While he won the wager, the officer was severely dealt with by his commanding officer and appeared in court the next day.

When the most destructive fire Glasgow ever experienced in the business section occurred at 2.57 pm on 14 October 1888, it was a miracle that the arcade was not reduced to a pile of rubble, as were the other three buildings involved in the fire.

Although the cause of the fire was a mystery, it started in a side stair near the hoist of R. Wylie Hill & Co.'s property in Buchanan Street, just above a sliding door separating it from the arcade. The rapidity with which the fire spread was the result of the flames being fanned by the draught in the hoist, which extended from the basement to the attic.

Simultaneous messages from St Enoch's fire station and the electric fire alarm at the Royal Exchange alerted the Fire Brigade. Available strength was at once turned out from the chief station but, when the brigade arrived a few minutes after the alarm was sounded, the three upper floors and the roof of the building were already alight. The fire quickly spread to the arcade's entrance and then to the rest of the building, part of the glass roof giving way under the heat. Both sides of the arcade suffered particularly and, on the south side, the upper storey was severely damaged, with the roof almost burned off. Luckily, the shops underneath were untouched by the flames, but the stock was ruined by the deluge of water. By evening, the arcade resembled a miniature canal.

After the fire, Stuart Cranston, the Glasgow man who invented the tearoom, took over the fire-damaged part of the arcade on the south side of the Buchanan Street entrance with the intention of turning it into a suite of tearooms and a dry-tea retailing shop. Opened in 1889, Cranston's new tearooms were the largest in the world. They had rooms for ladies only, a general tearoom, a gentlemen's tearoom and the largest, best-ventilated smoking room in the city. What was most ingenious however, was the installation of an early form of air conditioning. According to an advertisement, before being admitted to the salons, the fresh air was cleaned and deprived of all dust or smoke, heated in winter by hot-water pipes and cooled in summer by blocks of ice. Air from the rooms was expelled and replaced every 20 minutes by a continuous and imperceptible movement. The novelty of this innovation stimulated the public's curiosity and people came along in droves to test it.

Cranston opened another tearoom, at 43 Argyll Arcade, in 1892 and, in 1894, bought the whole arcade. Two years later Cranston Tea Rooms Limited was created and was made the owner of the arcade property rather than Cranston personally.

When Cranston bought the arcade, he laid down a strict code of conduct, that included regulating the design of shop fronts and the type of shop that could be opened. Each shopkeeper was subject to the code and conditions of title, which still apply today.

A new century dawned, and the tearooms were bursting at the seams,

The man who invented the tearoom, Stuart Cranston, opened the largest tearooms in the world in the arcade in 1889. By 1894 he owned the whole arcade

without room for further expansion. Cranston's remedy was to knock down the old mansion house in Buchanan Street fronting the arcade and replace it with a larger building. Not everyone was happy about this, and *The Glasgow Herald* carried a story entitled 'The Vanishing Face of Buchanan Street'. It reported that the building now being demolished, which formed the Buchanan Street entrance to the Argyll Arcade, was, with one exception, the only link between the past and the present of the street. The building had been to the new city what the Cross Steeple was to the old city – a favourite trysting place for visitors.

By 1904, the old mansion had been replaced by a red sandstone block designed in French Renaissance style by Colin Menzies. Argyll Arcade Buildings was advertised as being fireproof, and the letting agent's schedule stressed the quietness of the location, owing to Buchanan Street being paved with wood.

The new building provided the arcade with an imposing frontage – twin archways separated by a central pillar. At the top of each arch was a colourful mosaic, the left side spelling out 'Argyll Arcade' and the right showing a coat of arms with the date '1904'. Stuart Cranston's use of the coat of arms was unauthorised, as it belonged not to his family but to the barony of Cranstoun, which peerage had become extinct in 1869.

Although for a time Cranston Tea Rooms boomed, by 1919 money was tight and a year later the company was forced to sell parts of the arcade to the tenants to raise finance. (The business that Stuart Cranston had

The French Renaissance-style red sandstone block that in 1904 replaced the old mansion fronting the arcade

started went into voluntary liquidation in 1955.)

To look after the arcade business, it was arranged that there would be an annual meeting of the tenants at which a Committee of Management of five tenants would be elected that would have the power to make bye-laws for the regulation of matters falling within their jurisdiction. To this day, all shopkeepers must join the management committee, and any change in the appearance of their premises must be approved not only by Glasgow's local planning authority but by the committee.

Always on the lookout for novel methods of attracting custom to the arcade, the committee had a brainwave in 1931 – to string fairy lights from one end of the promenade to the other as Christmas decorations. By Christmas, 500 brightly coloured lights were in place and the arcade was said to be the first 'street' in Glasgow to use fairy lights in this way.

Advertising played an important part in the arcade's life, and in 1956 the committee came up with an innovative campaign to popularise it as Glasgow's finest shopping centre rather than as individual shops. The idea was to employ a 'hostess' as a liaison between the customer and the arcade,

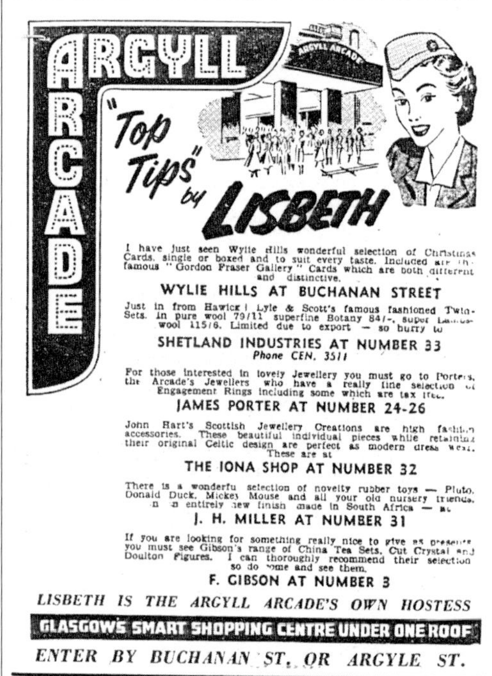

One of the advertisements appearing under the byline 'Top Tips' by LISBETH

which would attract custom for novelty value alone. Additional publicity would be gained by the hostess appearing in the press with celebrities who visited the arcade. Having been selected, the hostess was christened 'LIZBETH' and began featuring in a series of newspaper advertisements under the byline 'Top Tips' by LIZBETH.

Today most of the shops are jewellers, such as Porter's, the arcade's longest-surviving tenant, who first leased premises in 1887. However, as the original shopping layout was planned to ensure that a varied choice of quality goods was on sale, over the years there have been many well-loved shops trading under the elegant hammer-beam roof.

One of these was the Clyde Model Dockyard. Mention it to any man over 40 living in or around Glasgow and his eyes will light up before saying nostalgically, 'The Clyde Model Dockyard, oh yes, I remember …' Immediately visions are conjured up of Hornby trains, model planes, ships and cars, lead soldiers and, of course, that firm favourite, the Meccano set. The shop was every boy's dream and, although fathers would never have admitted it, they looked forward to a visit to the Dockyard just as much as their sons.

The Clyde Model Dockyard evolved from a business started by the arcade's first tenant, the Italian Antoni Galletti, an optician and looking-glass maker who progressed to making scientific instruments. When Antoni's son took over, he changed the direction of the business by making model engines, yachts and other novelties.

The next owner, Andrew McKnight, who was responsible for coining the celebrated name, continued what Antoni's son had started until the shop took the form that became so well known. In 1935, Wilson Taylor, whose slogan was 'The Shop of 1,000 Toys for Boys', bought the business and

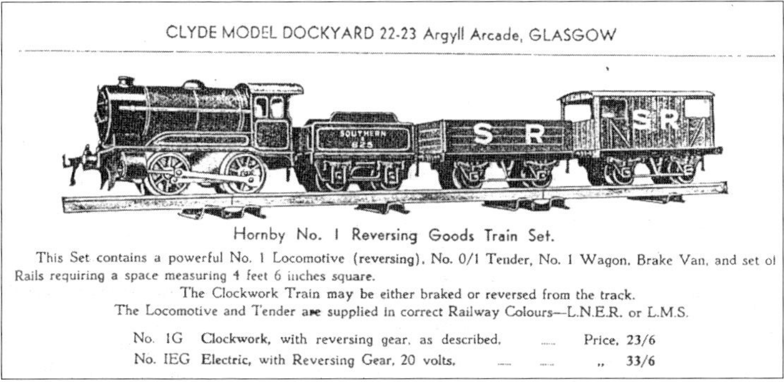

Early advertisement for the Clyde Model Dockyard

continued trading until 1972, when the iniquitous level of rates being charged on the property made it impossible for him to carry on.

For the feminine side of the family there was the Dolls' House, which had the largest variety of high-class dolls in the West of Scotland and, since the early 1900s, was famous as the Dolls' Hospital, the place where little girls brought their dolls to be repaired.

Another shop that is still remembered is that of Mrs Diack, which sold children's clothing. Aberdeen-born Catherine Diack was an amazing woman. She hated housework, and being confined to the house, and despite having nine children, she was bored. Her solution was to start a small business in Crown Street in Glasgow, making and selling babies' and children's clothes – christening robes, layettes, dresses, coats, all hand-stitched and all exquisite. Catherine's business was an immediate success, and she started to look for larger premises. She chose premises in the Argyll Arcade and, in 1869, 'Mrs Diack Children's Outfitters' appeared on the fascia board above No. 58.

After the First World War, money was tight and custom-made clothing became too expensive. Besides, customers had begun to like the idea of looking in shop windows, choosing a garment and taking it home there and then rather than waiting for it to be made. As the mass production of children's clothing

The redoubtable Mrs Diack and her staff photographed outside Mrs Diack Children's Outfitters in the 1890s

improved, the sailor suits and beautifully pin-tucked hand-embroidered dresses disappeared, to be replaced with stock from outside suppliers.

Mrs Diack continued to take an interest in the business until her death at the age of 84. Another Catherine Diack followed in her footsteps and, when she died, another Catherine took over. Unfortunately, in the 1980s, after 38 years in the business, Margaret Diack ceased trading as she had no family to carry on the tradition. A treasured part of Glasgow and the arcade went with her.

Another shop in the arcade was that of R. Wylie Hill & Co. If a toy or a household article could not be found there, it was probably unavailable anywhere in Glasgow. Mr R. Wylie Hill started his retail business in the early 1880s in Argyle Street, specialising in Oriental merchandise, china and toys. In 1887, he moved into 20 Buchanan Street, adjoining the arcade, which was not a lucky move, as his store burned to the ground a year later. Mr Hill returned to a newly built 20 Buchanan Street, where business prospered so much that more space was urgently required. The most obvious solution was to take premises in the arcade next door and shops Nos. 37–41 were added to the company's letterhead.

Wylie Hill's produced special catalogues for every occasion – weddings, spring, holidays, autumn, Christmas. No event was missed, and the range of goods was astonishing. There were dolls' houses and prams for girls, forts and building bricks for boys, handbags and bric-à-brac for women and attaché cases and wallets for men. Also available were china, crystal, furniture, fancy goods and light fittings. In fact, it would be easier to list what was not there. When Cranston's Tea Tooms gave up their property in 1954, Wylie Hill took it over, making them the largest tenant in the arcade. Wylie Hill closed its doors in the 1970s. High rates and difficulties had made it impossible to continue trading and another famous name disappeared from the Glasgow shopping scene.

Today, of the 35 outlets in the arcade all but two are jewellers. The Body Shop and Sloan's Restaurant nestle among the glittering array of gems on sale.

That concludes the historic trio. As already stated, their stories are interwoven, starting with Morrison's Court, where John Morrison had his coffee house, which became Sloan's Restaurant, and where John Reid had his timber yard, which became the site of the Argyll Arcade.

CHAPTER 21

SAUCHIEHALL STREET'S HIDDEN HOUSES

Albany Place Townhouses

It would probably surprise most people to discover that the north side of Sauchiehall Street between Scott Street and Charing Cross has not one, but six, hidden houses, relics of the street's original early 19th century houses, which were set in gardens and which were either demolished or engulfed by new buildings as the city grew westwards.

Some of the hidden houses are tucked away behind Albany Chambers at Charing Cross. They are all that remain entire of Albany Place, a terrace of town houses built in 1825, Albany Chambers being built on their front gardens. It is impossible to see the houses from either Sauchiehall Street or Renfrew Street, and the only way of approaching them is by the entrance to Albany Chambers at 534 Sauchiehall Street. Through a door on the first landing, there is a short flight of steps leading to a platform in front of the houses.

The houses look rather odd and are more like cottages than the three-

Albany Place as it was when built

storey houses they are said to have been. Apparently, this is because their lower floors were incorporated into the foundations and basement of Albany Chambers and what remains is the upper floor, doors having been created out of windows. Of the Albany Place houses, only three remain lived in but dilapidated. At one time, the Royal School of Shorthand was in the centre house, the premises of the Standing Conference for Women in the left and the Margaret Hopkins School of Dancing in the right, where, for more than a generation, little girls were taught the graceful art. The toilets in the dancing school were rather grand, being decorated with an entwined rose design. During a class one day, a child continually dashed out of the room to visit the toilets and, on being asked why she needed to go so often, replied, 'I go to see the "woses".'

Another Albany Place house has been incorporated into 518 Sauchiehall Street, the Royal Highland Fusiliers' Regimental Headquarters and Museum (see Chapter 22). Fortunately, this house has not been truncated, and although most of the rooms are used for offices, etc., the original staircase is intact and what was the drawing room is now the regimental mess. The room has rich pink walls, Georgian panels outlined in white, the original fireplace and a columned screen, all of which provide an elegant setting for regimental dinners, when the table groans under the weight of the regimental silver.

Hidden house No. 5 can be found near Strathclyde University's Baird Hall of Residence. It's a once-imposing detached villa, which has been incorporated into Scotland's largest nightclubs, the Garage, fronting on to Sauchiehall Street, and forms the G2 club at the rear. An ugly tunnel connects the two buildings, hiding the villa's Greek Doric portico.

What's left of Albany Place today

The once imposing detached villa that is hidden by the shops in Sauchiehall Street. It has been incorporated into the Garage nightclub which fronts on to Sauchiehall Street

Despite the villa being surrounded by additions, it is possible to mark out its perimeter from the inside. However, apart from pillars in what was the hall and two fireplaces in what was the drawing room but is now the bar, there is nothing left to show how it looked originally. Rooms have been divided and windows blocked up, and while there is a staircase in the original position, it is a replacement.

The nightclub's car park was once the yard of monumental sculptors John Gray & Company, the firm said to have repaired the Stone of Destiny when it was broken during its unofficial removal from Westminster Abbey to Scotland in 1950. All that remains of the yard is the platform upon which the crane that lifted all the heavy stones sat.

The last hidden house can be glimpsed only through a narrow opening in Scott Street. Having gone unnoticed for decades, it is a detached villa that was extended towards Scott Street. Its basement was also extended, so that the house was elevated on columns. Its garden was built on, the most significant building being the Grecian Building designed by Alexander 'Greek' Thomson, which faced on to Sauchiehall Street. This building was also extended with a brick-built warehouse on its west wing. Over the years all these buildings have been subdivided, added to and linked with a series of badly constructed low-level roofs.

Glasgow's Centre for Contemporary Arts, housed in the Grecian Building, is having a £10.5 million refurbishment, the centrepiece of which will be the hidden villa. Architects Page and Page won the design competition for the refurbishment, based on stripping the crude additions to reveal the original core buildings, which will be linked by a series of independent bridges to provide a 'promenade' around the new art centre. As once people could walk through the garden surrounding the villa, they will be able to walk around the 'cultural garden' surrounding the newly revealed villa. The villa, the rear elevation to the Grecian Building and the brick warehouse building will form the surrounding elevations to an enclosed courtyard with a high-level glazed roof.

When the project is finished, the public will get a chance to see one of the city's hidden gems – a 19th-century town house.

CHAPTER 22

THE SECRET OF 518 SAUCHIEHALL STREET

Royal Highland Fusiliers' Museum

The building belonging to the Royal Highland Fusiliers at 518 Sauchiehall Street has two secrets, the Albany Place house already mentioned in Chapter 21 and something else, which will be revealed as the history of the building unfolds.

It is a threefold history, covering photography, architecture and militaria, and although the building was built in 1904, its story really started 49 years earlier, in 1855, when the engraver Thomas Annan and a young doctor called Berwick set up a photography business at 68 Woodlands Road, Glasgow. Despite Berwick leaving shortly after the partnership was formed, by 1859 Annan was successful enough to open his own photographic printing works at Burnbank Road, Hamilton, from where he published views of 'Glasgow Cathedral' and 'Days on the Coast'. However, it was his series 'The

The outside of 518 Sauchiehall Street

Old Closes and Streets of Glasgow', taken between 1868 and 1871, that brought him world acclaim. (At the time Glasgow had made a historic and momentous decision to rid itself of the privately owned disease-ridden overcrowded slums housing most of its citizens and had commissioned Annan to photograph them for posterity.)

When Thomas Annan died in 1887, his sons carried on the business and, on moving into 153 Sauchiehall Street, as well as taking photographs, they held fine art exhibitions, such as those of the Glasgow Art Club and the Royal Scottish Water Colour Society. In 1892 another move was made to 230 Sauchiehall Street and thanks to the profitability of the company's appointment as official photographers to the 1901 Glasgow International Exhibition, it was possible to build new premises in keeping with its high profile in the photography world – 518 Sauchiehall Street, a narrow four-storey red-sandstone gabled building designed by John Keppie and Charles Rennie Mackintosh.

T. & R. Annan moved into its new home in 1904 and stayed there until 1959, when what was then the War Department bought it as a regimental headquarters and museum for the Royal Highland Fusiliers, the regiment formed that year by the amalgamation of the Royal Scots Fusiliers and the Highland Light Infantry.

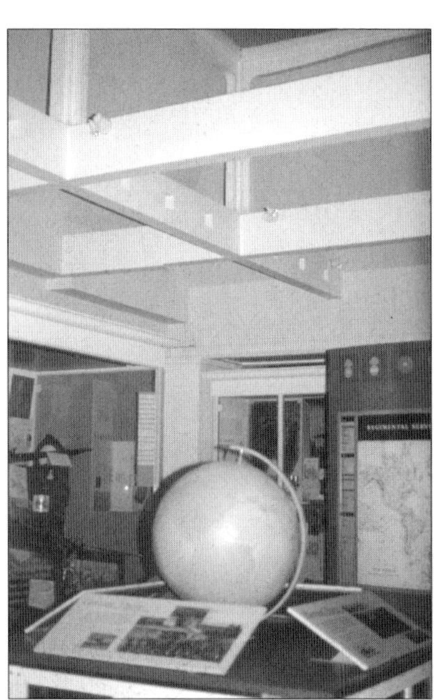

Mackintosh's square pierced beams

A treasure house of militaria, the museum was completely redesigned in 1997 in line with today's idea of bringing history alive with interactive displays. As well as having one of the best collections of militaria in Scotland, the museum tells the story, often chilling, of the officers and men who served the regiment around the world, recounting, often in their own words, their experiences. The ground floor covers 1678 to the Boer War, the top floors the two World Wars to the present day.

While the outside of the building seems to be all Keppie, showing his liking for sculpture in the two sibyls (an ancient prophetess or witch), inside is definitely the work of Mackintosh, which brings us to the secret of the building – Mackintosh square pierced beams and Mackintosh wrought-iron decorations on the magnificent lift shaft. The area, now the part of the museum explaining the origins of the regiment, was originally T. & R. Annan's ground-floor gallery and the lift took clients up to the photographic studio on the first floor. (T & R Annan has a fine set of original interior pictures among which are views of its ground-floor gallery with its Mackintosh beams and graceful lift shaft.)

The museum is open Monday to Thursday from 9.30 am to 4.30 pm and on Fridays from 9.30 am to 4 pm. Entry is free, and the building is well worth a visit.

Mackintosh's magnificent wrought-iron lift shaft

CHAPTER 23

A TOUCH OF OLD ENGLAND

Sunlight Cottages, Kelvingrove Park

There is a touch of Old England hidden in the heart of the city – two picturesque cottages in Kelvingrove Park teetering on a steep bank above the River Kelvin. They are all that remain of the 1901 International Exhibition and were presented to the city by Lord Leverhulme after the exhibition closed.

Designed by James Miller, the architect responsible for all the exhibition's buildings, the cottages were modelled on one of the blocks of houses at Lever Brothers' model township of Port Sunlight in Cheshire. (Miller began his architectural career as a designer for the Caledonian Railway and many of his stations were in the English half-timbered style. His Botanic Gardens Station, now demolished, had the familiar half-timbering and red-brick walls but was tinged with an Oriental flavour, having two tall turrets on the roof with gilded onion-shaped domes. At the time, it was described as 'a strange sight in Glasgow'.)

Two storeys high, the Sunlight Cottages have multi-gables decorated with carved timber bargeboards, multi-paned windows, boldly detailed chimneys and red-tiled roofs. The walls are of bright red brick, which, with the black-and-white half-timbering, provides a picturesque taste of an idealised England.

The picturesque Sunlight Cottages, all that remains in situ *of the 1901 International Exhibition*

Owned by Glasgow City Council but in the care of the Parks Department, the cottages are occupied by Council gardeners.

CHAPTER 24

THE OLDEST HOUSE IN THE MERCHANT CITY

42 Miller Street

The oldest house in the Merchant City is tucked away in the middle of the east side of Miller Street, looking slightly out of place among its tall neighbours. It is No. 42 and is the last of the so-called Virginia tobacco merchants' houses to survive entire. Palladian in style, it was designed by John Craig in 1775 and built on ground feued from the house garden of John Miller, a maltman. The design was influenced by Miller's regulations that 'each house must consist of a half-sunk and two square storeys, no gables, chimneys of "corbie steps" facing the street and entered by a front door and flight of steps projected on the intended pavement . . .' In addition there was to be no brewing, tanning of leather, making of candles or soap or any other business that could be 'nauseous' or 'hurtful' to the inhabitants of Miller Street.

No. 42's first inhabitants were the leading Glasgow merchant family of Robert Findlay, whose son, also Robert, was Dean of Guild 1796–97 and a member of the Trades House and the Chamber of Commerce. To distinguish Robert Junior from his father, he was known as 'Robert the Banker'. As was the custom among the city's merchants, the counting house for their business was in their home and the iron safes for these transactions still exist. The house was sold out of the family in 1826 and, in 1836, it was inherited by the Misses Brown of Paisley, becoming the offices for the City and Suburban Gas Company until 1866. Thereafter, it was occupied by a succession of jewellers, glass importers, cotton spinners, printers and a mantle manufacturer and, at one time, it belonged to the Thistle Bank.

From 1989, the building lay derelict and slowly decaying while the area around it saw refurbishment and renewal. Help was on hand, however, and, in 1992 the Virginia Court Development Company offered the building to the Glasgow Building Preservation Trust for £1. Following a detailed feasibility study on its condition and potential for re-use, a funding package was put together to enable the building both to regain its original elegant neoclassical appearance and to contribute through its proposed use to the regeneration of Glasgow's city centre.

When the Glasgow Building Preservation Trust first saw No. 42, the original fine ashlar façade was hidden under thick coats of paint that had weathered, causing the stone beneath to erode. A clumsy and ugly mansard roof had been added, Victorian single-pane sash-and-case windows had replaced the original multi-pane variety, and the swagged stone urns that had decorated the wall head until the late 19th century had vanished. Internally, little survived apart from some simple stone fireplace surrounds, some panelled doors and fragmentary evidence of plasterwork on the ground floor, all of which were used as a basis for remodelling.

Despite everything, No. 42 was still recognisable as a Georgian villa of classical Palladian-style design, with its advanced centre bay and distinctive Corinthian pilastered doorway. The ground floor was raised above a semi-sunk basement, which originally had pavement grilles that had long since been covered over. (Thanks to a grant from the Glasgow Development Agency, artist Jack Sloan was commissioned to design a series of cast-iron grilles to replace those missing.)

The restoration of the building began in October 1994 and was completed by the following October, when the Glasgow Building Preservation Trust moved into the ground floor, becoming its first new occupants.

The house during the 1970s, when it was neglected and occupied by assorted tenants. The clock, which has No. 42 printed on its face, today hangs above one of the building's fireplaces

Externally, the restoration attempted to reinstate exactly the original appearance of the building by rediscovering the natural stone façade and using crown glass in the windows. Inside, new plasterwork and joinery were reproduced to original profiles and the original room layout recreated, forming modern offices. No. 42 is now a Grade A-listed building of 'national importance', and its restoration received a Heritage Award from Historic Scotland.

With grant assistance provided by the Heritage Lottery Fund and generous loan facilities by a private foundation, the Scottish Civic Trust acquired the building in 1997. Founded in 1967, the trust is a charity receiving a government grant for fulfilling certain practical functions. Although it also receives local-authority support, more than half its income is dependent on covenants from industry, commerce, the professions and private individuals throughout Scotland. The trust's function is to help give listed buildings a meaningful new lease of life. It also coordinates the Scottish programme of Doors Open Day, part of the European Heritage Days Initiative.

No. 42 is fully tenanted, with the Glasgow Building Preservation Trust on the ground floor alongside the new Conservation Centre, Strathclyde Building Preservation Trust on the second floor and two other environment-related organisations in the basement. To mark the acquisition by the Scottish Civic Trust, HRH The Prince of Wales, Patron of the Scottish Civic Trust, opened the building on 28 January 1998 by unveiling a commemorative plaque.

Now you know the history of the old building, you might be interested

The house after restoration, which returned it to its original state, the ugly mansard roof that had been added having been removed. The restoration of the building, which is now Grade A-listed, received a Heritage Award from Historic Scotland

to know a little about Miller Street (1771). The ground on which it was opened formed part of the Langcroft and, early in the 17th century, a great part of the ground belonged to two sisters called Janet and Peggy Watson. In 1647, they sold their land to John Woodrow, a maltman in Glasgow who gradually purchased a large portion of the adjoining ground. More than a century later, his grandson, John Miller, inherited his estate and, soon afterwards, purchased the small portion of ground remaining, enabling him to own the whole of the Miller Street area.

Mr Miller was, like his grandfather, a maltman, his brewery being in the village of Grahamston, now the site of Central Station. When he inherited the Langcroft land, he demolished the malt kiln and thatched barn at what is now the foot of the south-east corner of Miller Street and Argyle Street and replaced them with a mansion house for himself whose gardens reached up to Ingram Street.

After living in his house for a few years, the opening of new streets gave Miller the idea of feuing his garden for a similar purpose, as others had done so profitably. When he consulted a surveyor, however, he was advised to demolish his house, as it would be in the way. Miller rejected this suggestion on the grounds of needless extravagance but later, when told that the entrance to the street would be inadequate if he did not take down at least half his house, he agreed that one wing could go. While that helped, it still made Miller Street narrower than its neighbours.

Miller may not have been fussy about the width of the street but he was about its appearance. As already mentioned, the houses had to conform to a fixed plan and, so as to preserve the residential character of the street, shops were strictly forbidden. His intention was to close the street at the top, as he did not want it to become a thoroughfare for carts, but when the residents applied to have it paved and lit by the Council, their request was refused because of the gate and wall at the north end. After it was agreed that the street could be used as a public highway, the Council gave it pavements and lights.

Stirling's Library began its life at No. 48 Miller Street, which was built on the site of the original No. 7, the home of Walter Stirling, who left money to establish the first free library in Scotland.

CHAPTER 25

THE LADY WELL
Public Well, Ladywell Street

Our next subject, a relic of old Glasgow, is hidden by way of being off the beaten track, which is why few people know about it. It can be found on the north side of what is left of Ladywell Street and is a niche containing a cast-iron urn topped by a pediment and a cross. The niche marks the site of the Lady Well, one of the 16 public wells referred to by Glasgow's first historian, M'Ure, as being in existence in 1726. The Lady Well (Well of Our Lady) was said to have been for the use of the common people who were not allowed to use the nearby Priests' Well.

In those days Glasgow's water supply was obtained from the River Clyde and public wells. The former was better suited for washing clothes, etc., but was used only by those who could afford to employ servants or others to do this work. A few families had private wells but, generally, the inhabitants

The Lady Well in Ladywell Street

had to resort to the wells in the public streets, which were sufficient for their ordinary requirements because there were no built-in baths or any of the other conveniences considered indispensable today. It was an everyday sight, morning and evening, to see the wells surrounded by housewives and maidservants, with their stoups (wooden buckets) set down in rows, waiting their turn to be served. On Saturdays there was extra pressure, as a supply had to be provided for that day and for Sunday.

As the Lady Well lay in a hollow, polluted surface water constantly gravitated towards it, making it a sanitary danger to the houses gradually spreading around it. Furthermore, after the Necropolis was built, it was thought that the source of the spring had been tainted because of its nearness to the graves. In deference to this fear, the well was stoned up around 1820.

A plaque on the well states that it was restored in 1836, rebuilt by the Merchants' House in 1874 and restored again in 1983 by Tennent Caledonian Breweries.

The Lady Well gave the street (one of the city's most ancient paths since it led to the cathedral) its name.

CHAPTER 26

THE TENEMENT HOUSE
145 Buccleuch Street, Garnethill

There's nothing about the façade of the red-sandstone tenement building at 145 Buccleuch Street in Garnethill to suggest it hides a first-floor flat that has remained in a time warp. The flat, known as the Tenement House, belongs to the National Trust for Scotland and is exceptional because it has never been altered and retains all its original fittings apart from gas lighting, which the Trust restored. The fact that it is in a building still lived in by other families adds to its uniqueness.

Built in 1892, the Tenement House is one of 56 similar flats within a massive structure of seven stairs, or 'closes' as Glaswegians call them. It has a hall, parlour, bedroom, kitchen and bathroom, which would have been considered generous and well equipped by the standards of the day, as it was usual for whole families to occupy flats the size of the kitchen at 145 Buccleuch Street. These were the single ends, the one-room houses that made Victorian and Edwardian Glasgow notorious.

145 Buccleuch Street with the Tenement House on the first floor (Photograph by Courtesy of National Trust for Scotland)

Despite being open to the public, the Tenement House is not a museum but was the home of an ordinary Glasgow citizen who lived there from 1911 to 1965. Her name was Agnes Reid Toward, and she changed practically nothing in her home and surrounded herself with the accumulated trivia of a lifetime, much of which is exhibited at the house.

Although the furnishings and fittings of Miss Toward's flat present a fascinating picture of domestic life in the early 20th century, her personal 'treasures' – letters, newspaper cuttings, mementoes, postcards, recipes, bills, wartime leaflets, even her schoolbooks, give a unique detailed insight into everyday life over six decades. Her papers reveal even the smallest details of her life, for example, when she was a child she played with a doll called Rosa and had a cat called Tibs.

Agnes Toward

While the house is unique, the story it tells is of an ordinary Glasgow woman who lived in an ordinary Glasgow tenement.

Agnes Toward was born in 1886 in Renfrew Street, the daughter of Agnes Reid and William Toward, a metal merchant. She was an only child, a younger sister dying in infancy. Her father died when she was only three, and Agnes was brought up by her mother, a dressmaker who also took in lodgers. Her mother had owned a small draper's shop in St Vincent Street but had had to give it up when she became ill, which is when she turned to dressmaking at home. Judging by the dress of the people in family photographs and the fact that Agnes' father employed 'four hands', the family seemed to be fairly well-to-do before Mr Toward's death.

Agnes' education began at Garnethill Public School and continued at Woodside Higher Grade School. Most children left school at the age of 14 but, being a bright pupil, Agnes stayed on until she was nearly 16 and then studied shorthand and typing at the Athenaeum Commercial College in Buchanan Street.

When Agnes and her mother moved into 145 Buccleuch Street in 1911, she was 25 and was a shorthand typist with Miller & Richards, a shipping firm in Union Street. When Miller & Richards moved to London in 1914, she went to work for Prentice, Service & Henderson, another shipping firm. She was one of the first two women ever employed by the company. They were taken on because of the outbreak of the First World War and were expected to give up their jobs when the men from the office came back. Agnes remained there until she retired in 1959 at the age of 73.

Agnes never married, and, after her mother died in 1939, she lived in the spacious house on her own. She did all her own housework, baked cakes, made jam and hardly ever threw out any of her own or her family's possessions.

Miss Toward led an active life. She liked music and dancing, going to the theatre and taking part in office activities, like a ladies' night out in 1958 to the King's Theatre to see the Kenneth McKellar show *Old Chelsea*, with Richard Tauber's music. At home she wrote long newsy letters to friends and listened to her battery wireless, bought in 1940, probably to get news of the Second World War. She was a regular member of Wellington Church in Southpark Avenue and attended meetings of the Women's Guild. In elections she voted Conservative.

Apart from redecorating, the only major change Miss Toward made to her flat was when she had electricity installed in 1960, paid for by the Wellington Church Kirk Session Benevolent Fund. She had thought about it as far back as 1935, as a letter to a friend shows:

> I have been thinking a little about putting in electric light – the cost, however, might be £25. Besides, I am told there are so many formalities to go through and the factors might insist I employ their contractors to do the job. You see, I know somebody who knows an engineer who might do the work for me and whom I could trust to leave in the house in the evening, or Saturday afternoon. I am afraid I will have to be content with the old gas, but I do get exasperated with the poor light in the kitchen in the winter and am afraid I say quite nasty things when I go into presses or the rooms without my torch.

After retiring, Agnes became increasingly unable to look after herself and, in 1965, was taken into hospital, where she remained until her death ten years later.

No. 145 Buccleuch Street was preserved by pure chance. In her will Miss Toward had left six chairs to her church elder, Sam Davidson, a regular visitor over the years, and, when he went to the house to collect them, his niece, actress Anna Davidson, came with him. Anna was fascinated by the house, which looked as if it had been frozen in time and, on hearing that the landlord wanted to clear and modernise it, was so horrified that she bought it and its contents. She then moved in and made it habitable while preserving its unique period character. As the house had lain empty for ten years and was dirty and neglected, Anna Davidson said that the first time she saw it, she felt like Pip in *Great Expectations*, when he stood at the door of the room Miss Havisham had occupied as a recluse for so many years.

Seven years later, in 1982, Anna left Glasgow and, wishing to see the house and its contents preserved, sold it to the National Trust for Scotland, who, after some restoration, opened it to the public the following year.

Although Anna Davidson realised what a valuable piece of social history she had saved from destruction, it was only after the National Trust bought the property that it became known just what a valuable part of Scotland's heritage it was, as Miss Toward had rarely thrown anything out. The house was crammed with all sorts of things that most people discard daily and, by studying them, it was possible to reconstruct Miss Toward's life, resulting in a Trust publication, *Miss Toward of The Tenement House*. Many of the fascinating documents of social history are displayed at 145 Buccleuch Street in the two ground-floor flats, bought by the Trust for the purpose.

Walking into the Tenement House is like taking a step back in time to the Edwardian age. It is almost as Miss Toward would have known it, as most of the furniture is hers and the gas lighting, which had been replaced by electricity, has been reinstalled. Each room has been decorated in the period of the house, and specimens of the original wallpaper are displayed. There is

The bedroom with its iron-and-brass bed covered with a typical white cotton bed mat (Photograph by Courtesy of National Trust for Scotland)

even a plaque on the stairway saying 'MRS TOWARD, DRESSMAKING, NO FITTING REQUIRED, First Flat'.

As has already been mentioned, the flat has a parlour, bedroom, kitchen and bathroom, all leading off a spacious hall. Of the hall's furnishings, the bamboo umbrella stand belongs to the house, as does the oil painting, probably of Miss Toward's grandfather, who is thought to have owned the grandfather clock and the Scotch chest, a piece of furniture once found in many Scottish households. The middle drawer of the top three – known as a 'lum' drawer – was used for storing top hats (or 'lum hats'). Still hanging in the hall is Miss Toward's gas mask from the Second World War. She had covered with cloth.

The bedroom has a black cast-iron fireplace and a traditional iron-and-brass bedstead, with a framed text on the wall above, common then in God-fearing Scottish homes. A set of jugs and a basin sit on top of a marble-topped washstand and, among the personal objects on the dressing table, are glass perfume bottles. On top of the wardrobe are suitcases Miss Toward would have used when she went on her annual holiday. (As an office worker, she was one of the lucky people who, early in the 20th century, had holidays with pay. Until the late 1930s many people had no paid annual holidays. Like most Glasgow people at the time, Miss Toward preferred to spend her holidays at one of the Clyde Coast resorts, particularly Largs. A receipt for 1942 tells that it cost her £7.0.0 for 14 days' board and lodgings at the Dunedin.)

Miss Toward's very comfortable parlour with the box bed in the corner (Photograph by Courtesy of National Trust for Scotland)

Traditionally, parlours were used only on special occasions such as weddings and funerals, and Miss Toward would have lit the fire in the white marble fireplace only when someone important was calling – possibly the minister or a kirk elder. Agnes' mother bought the overmantel in 1917 from a shop in nearby Elderslie Street. It cost £1.10s. Intended for summoning a maid, the white china bell-handle was standard in all the houses when they were built, as labour was cheap and, although the Towards did not employ a servant, many families in Buccleuch Street did.

Most of the furniture in the parlour is mahogany, and some pieces, such as the Pembroke table and the small writing desk, were inherited by Miss Toward from her father's family. The oval table, draped with a chenille cover and white tablecloth, is set for afternoon tea. There is also a sewing machine, made in America about 1860, which probably belonged to Mrs Toward, and a rosewood piano with Miss Toward's sheet music stacked on top – Scottish ballads, popular songs and dances from the turn of the century. Behind the door in the corner, the set-in bed was an economical way of providing extra sleeping accommodation. This was more or less a cupboard and is found only in houses built before 1900, when, for health reasons, they were banned.

With its large black range, coal bunker, sink with brass taps at the window, fitted shelves and a bed in the recess behind the door, the kitchen is typical of a Glasgow tenement kitchen. The range was used for cooking and provided hot water that was stored in a tank in a fireside cupboard and then piped to the kitchen sink and the bathroom. Coal was kept in the large bunker opposite the range, which was cleaned with Zebo, a black liquid polish that protected it from rust as well as making it gleam. Miss Toward was very attached to her range and, in a letter to a friend in 1935, said she was not taking it out although the craze was to have interior fireplaces and cookers in the kitchen.

Ironing was done on the kitchen table using flatirons heated on the range. Baking was also done on the table using the utensils displayed. Miss Toward's papers revealed that she wrote down the results of her recipes, noting what went wrong and how it could have been avoided. Among the cooking tools on the shelves are jelly pans and earthenware pots that Miss Toward used when making jam. In a cupboard there are even some uneaten pots of jam, the oldest labelled 'Plum 1929'.

While the kitchen is typical of a Glasgow tenement, the bathroom is not, as, when 145 Buccleuch Street was built, few Glaswegians had the luxury of a toilet in their own flat. Most tenement dwellers shared an outside privy with their neighbours. The 1892 Act compelling landlords to provide indoor water closets was not entirely effective, as some tenements still had outside toilets in the 1950s.

A bathroom, especially one with a window, was found only in the best-appointed houses and, by the standards of the day, the one in the Tenement House would have been considered luxurious, with its deep bath with brass fittings, a marble-effect washbasin and a toilet with a wooden seat and china-handled pullchain. The window shelf holds a fascinating assortment of pill boxes, medicine bottles of the day and a brass can used for carrying hot water to the wash-stand in the bedroom. It's likely the Towards had not always lived in a house with an inside bathroom, as they brought the bedroom wash-stand with them when they moved to Buccleuch Street.

That concludes a visit to the Tenement House, a building as fascinating and important as the grandest of mansions in the contribution it makes to our knowledge of the past. In fact, as tenements and Glasgow are synonymous, it now seems strange that a tenement house had not been preserved *in situ* earlier.

A typical Edwardian kitchen with range, and pulley for hanging up wet washing (Photograph by Courtesy of National Trust for Scotland)

CHAPTER 27

REMAINS OF THE TWELFTH-CENTURY CATHEDRAL

The Lower Church, Glasgow Cathedral

That a building such as Glasgow Cathedral, dating from 1233, could in any way be considered as part of 'Hidden Glasgow' would never occur to most people. They would be wrong, however, as hidden inside are remains of the first stone church built in 1197 by Bishop Jocelyn, who gave us the Glasgow Fair holiday.

These remains can be found in the beautiful Lower Church, a particularly fine example of medieval Scottish architecture and the most distinctive feature of the Cathedral. As it is not below ground level, the Lower Church is not a crypt, although it is often wrongly so called. In the first bay and a half of the south aisle there is a single vaulting shaft with distinctive late-12th-century decoration set against the remains of an east wall of the same date. Later, an arch was cut through this east wall, giving access to the south aisle. The vaulting shaft and remains of the vestibule's east wall are the only parts of the 1197 building still in their original place.

The vestibule is thought to have been a temporary chapel for the shrine of St Kentigern while the eastern arm of the Cathedral was being built in the 13th century. In the vestibule is a lid of a tomb chest, thought to date from about 1200, with ornamented edges and a very worn outline of a figure.

Why Jocelyn's vaulting shaft was left standing has long been the subject of debate. Various theories have been offered, one being that in the 13th century, it was common to enlarge the choir by extending it eastwards and adding a lady chapel, which might have made it unnecessary for a new and formal consecration of the new structure – an addition being different from a reconstruction.

A much more feasible theory, however, is expounded by Thomas Lennox Watson in his book *The Double Choir of Glasgow Cathedral*, published in 1916. According to him, the pillar is not in its original place, as it is inconsistent with any possible plan of an earlier building on the site of the present one. The capital is disproportionate to the height of the shaft and its carving is of a later date than the moulding of the abacus and the base of the shaft. The pillar is a contradiction of everything in its vicinity, despite the top bed of the capital being in line with the top of the other capitals and the bench on which it stands being on the level of the bench of the south wall. To Watson, these irregularities proved conclusively that the pillar is not *in situ*.

Why is it there, then? Watson's reasoning is that, when it was decided to pull down Jocelyn's church and erect a new cathedral on the site, it was necessary to provide a resting place for the bones of St Kentigern, where masses and other services might be performed daily over his body. When the plans of the new cathedral were drawn up therefore, a section of the south aisle of the new building was designated for that purpose.

A corner of the old choir was pulled down and the south-west compartment of the new lower church constructed in its place. This small chapel, for that was what it was to be during the erection of the new choir,

Glasgow Cathedral in 1957

was designed as part of the south aisle of the lower church and was vaulted and roofed over at the level of the choir floor. A recessed altar was built against the west wall, and beneath the altar were laid the relics of the saint.

Although, quite naturally, the builders wanted to give the shrine to the saint some architectural adornment, the temporary nature of the altar prevented vast expenditure on it. Despite the lack of funds, however, the builders achieved their objective by recycling material from the part of Jocelyn's church that they had just pulled down. Using the old stones, they constructed a pillar on each side of the altar recess and arches above the pillars and in front of the recess.

Later, when the vaulting of the temporary chapel was taken down and rebuilt to the original design, one of the pillars and a portion of the altar were incorporated into the new structure as a memento of the chapel and Jocelyn's church. To give the pillar some show of useful function, a vaulting rib was carried from its capital to the crown of the reconstructed vault.

Watson's theory makes sense, because, as he says, it is just not believable that the new cathedral was designed to accommodate itself to the levels of an insignificant fragment of the earlier building. Nor was it feasible to assume a double coincidence of levels of the earlier and later wall shafts. To

Bishop Jocelyn's vaulting shaft of the 12th century, set against the remains of an east wall of the same date. Note the different size and shape of the pillar's capital compared to the one on the pillar to the right

Watson, either supposition was absurd.

The only other reminder of the 12th-century church is a *voussoir*, a wedge-shaped stone from an arch, plastered and painted on two sides, which is displayed in the Chapel of St John the Evangelist. It's one of the only two known examples surviving of the art of wall painting in medieval Scotland, and was found in 1916 in the filling above the mid-13th-century vault of the Lower Church. As the pattern, an inverted heart with two lobes near the base and a spray of *palmette* foliage springing from between them, was popular with stone painters in the latter part of the 12th century, the stone is presumed to be have been part of the east end of the church, dedicated in 1197.

Alongside the *voussoir* is St Mungo's Well, which supplied water to the early monastic community. Although lifting the lid and peering down the well shows no sign of water, it is said to be there, about 15 feet down.

On the north aisle of the Lower Church is the Covenanters' Memorial, a stone commemorating nine Covenanters who were hanged and beheaded at Glasgow Cross between 1666 and 1688 for their stand against the Restoration and Episcopacy. The stone formerly marked the Covenanters' graves in the churchyard but was placed inside the church for preservation. After giving the names of the nine victims, the inscription goes on:

Voussoir – (a painted wedge-shaped stone from the 12th-century church)

Years sixty six and eighty four
Did send their souls home into glore,
Whose bodies here enterred ly,
Then sacrificed to tyranny,
To Covenants and Reformation,
'Cause they adhered in their station.
These nine, with others in this yard,
Whose heads and bodies were not spar'd,
Their testimonies, foes to bury,
Caused beat the drum then in great fury.
They'll know at resurrection day
To murder saints was no sweet play!

However, there is still a memorial in the churchyard commemorating the Covenanters. It is hidden above the boiler house north of the cathedral and gives the names of the nine men 'who all suffered at the Cross of Glasgow for their testimony to the Covenants'.

Alongside the Covenanters' Memorial inside the cathedral are two carved stones with a plaque saying, 'These stones from a doorway of the former Bishop's Castle were placed here in 1965. Below the Arms of James V, King of Scots, are those of Gavin Dunbar, Archbishop of Glasgow 1524–47 and of James Houston, sub dean.' The castle and its grounds occupied much of the area covered by the present Cathedral Square, west of the Cathedral and to the south of the front of the Royal Infirmary.

For more than 1,500 years, the site of the Cathedral has been held sacred, for there the Cross was planted and the ground was blessed for Christian burial by St Ninian (397). The cathedral is Crown property but, the congregation that worships in it belongs to the Church of Scotland.

CHAPTER 28

MACKINTOSH HIDDEN IN A LANE

20–28 Renfield Lane

Only in Glasgow could you find a Charles Rennie Mackintosh building hidden down a lane only 18 feet wide and in perpetual shadow. The building, which is in Renfield Lane, near Central Station, was designed by Mackintosh in 1899 for the *Daily Record* newspaper, founded in 1895. For a paper that was the first halfpenny morning newspaper in Britain to use photography and

Charles Rennie Mackintosh's drawing for Daily Record buildings in Renfield Lane (right)

print ten text pages while its front page carried news and advertisements, it is understandable it would want someone innovative, like Mackintosh, to design its new building. (At the time, Mackintosh worked for Honeyman & Keppie and had already designed *The Glasgow Herald* building in Mitchell Street, now the Lighthouse.)

Construction lasted from 1900 to 1906, although the building was in use from May 1901, when only the basement and three upper floors were complete. What makes the building particularly interesting is that it shows the architect's handling of an awkward elevational problem. He skilfully overcame the restrictions of the site, fronted by narrow Renfield Lane and encased between other commercial properties. Furthermore, to compensate for the poorly lit site, his generous fenestration and the use of reflective white-glazed brick for the façade was inspirational. (This is the only building in which Mackintosh used brick as a facing material.)

The façade is well proportioned, with a stone-faced ground storey below the white brick. At fourth-floor level, there's a series of projecting bays and an attic storey with dormers in red sandstone. Mackintosh gave the hard white surface between the bays an interesting texture by projecting occasional coloured tiles as stylised trees. The many windows are attractively small-paned.

When Mackintosh's drawing for the building came into the possession of the Hunterian Museum, a black sticker covered the inscription at the bottom right, leaving only Mackintosh's name exposed. Until he became a recognised partner of Honeyman & Keppie in 1904, all work by him carried the name of the practice, not his alone, something Mackintosh clearly felt obliged to rectify later. The watercolour finish of the drawing is unique, as usually Mackintosh worked his perspectives in black ink to enable their easy reproduction in the architectural press.

In 1971, the *Daily Record* vacated the premises at 20–28 Renfield Lane, the interior of which has been altered.

CHAPTER 29

THE FORGOTTEN ROOMS

Trades House, Glassford Street

These are the forgotten rooms of the top floor of the Trades House in Glassford Street. They were once classrooms and have been in a time warp since the days when children learned and played in them. The original wooden floors remain untouched, as do the walls and ceilings.

The building, built in 1791, is the official home of the body known as the Trades House of Glasgow. Formed on 6 February 1605, this was originally a federal union of the 14 craft incorporations, the Scottish equivalent of the craft guilds that developed in most of the great cities of Europe in the Middle Ages. Today, the House concerns itself not just with the maintenance of tradition but also with the allocation of substantial funds for good causes.

The Trades School, which met in the forgotten rooms, was set up by the incorporations for their members' children at the beginning of the 19th century and continued until the coming of compulsory public education at

The old schoolroom, which lay in a time warp until 1999 when it was discovered at the top of the Trades House

the end of the 19th century. Just inside the Reception Room on the ground floor is a framed tapestry of Moses in the bulrushes worked by a child who attended the Trades School and presented by a descendant who first visited the House on a Doors Open Day.

Robert Adam designed the building, which is considered to be one of the seven most important buildings designed by him. The frontage is typically his, with three light windows enclosed within arches and, based on a Greek temple design, a central feature with twin Ionic columns. Surmounting the façade is a balustrade with a central frieze with Britannia as its main figure.

It is planned to turn the dusty classrooms into a banqueting and conference centre as part of a £2 million facelift of the Trades House, the oldest building in Glasgow, apart from the cathedral, still used for its original purpose. The Trades House has been backed by the National Lottery Fund in its effort to raise the money for its restoration and is optimistic of receiving £500,000 towards it.

CHAPTER 30

WHO IS THAT MAN?

Bust of Beethoven, Renfrew Street

Unless you are in the habit of walking along the Charing Cross end of Renfrew Street you probably have not come across the low red-sandstone building with a larger-than-lifesize bust of a man on it, also in red sandstone. If you have, you must have wondered who on earth the man is and why his bust was put on the building. That it is above what is obviously the back door of the building makes it even more curious and must make people wonder if the rear of the building was originally the front.

Research has revealed that the bust is that of Beethoven and is on the rear door of what was once the notable musical-instrument shop of Hepburn and Ross in Sauchiehall Street. The pianos came in by the back door and it seemed appropriate to the architect to have them pass under the bust of a great composer.

Beethoven adorning the rear of what was once the musical-instrument shop of Hepburn and Ross in Sauchiehall Street

CHAPTER 31

IT COULD ONLY HAPPEN IN GLASGOW

Lobey Dosser Statue, Woodlands Road

To anyone other than a Glaswegian, the city's most unusual monument is an enigma. It is a bronze statue of Lobey Dosser, the Sheriff of Calton Creek, astride his two-legged horse, El Fideldo, with his arch-enemy, Rank Badjin, perched on the saddle behind him.

Lobey Dosser was a cowboy strip cartoon created for the *Evening Times* by cartoonist and poet Bud Neill. Its surreal deadpan quality struck such a chord with readers that grown men waited anxiously for the next day's

The unique much loved statue of Lobey Dosser, the Sheriff of Calton Creek

paper to see how the plot was developing.

Lobey, who can be found in Woodlands Road, is the first statue to be erected by public subscription since Victorian times and resulted from a campaign to pay tribute in Glasgow's European Year of Culture to Bud, who was immensely popular in the 1950s and 1960s.

Once it had been decided that the tribute would take the form of a statue of Bud's famous cartoon characters, Lobey Dosser, El Fideldo and Rank Badjin, one of the campaigners, Tom Shields, asked the readers of his *Glasgow Herald* Diary column to help raise the money – £10,000 being the target.

The next task was to find someone who could make the statue. This didn't prove to be quite as easy as expected but, after a couple of disappointments, help came in the shape of Tony Morrow and Nick Gillan, two final-year sculpture students at Duncan of Jordanstone College of Art in Dundee.

With the problem of who would sculpt the statue out of the way, everything seemed to be on course until Tony and Nick said the £10,000 budget would be at least £8,000 short even though they did not charge for their work.

Again, the generous Glaswegians dipped their hands into their pockets, the extra money was raised and, in 1992, the statue of Lobey Dosser, El Fideldo and Rank Badjin was erected in memory of Bud Neill, a local hero.

The people of Glasgow have really taken to the bronze Lobey, and Elfie (the two-legged horse) has a shiny nose from being affectionately rubbed. It is highly entertaining to watch the bewildered look on the faces of tourists who come across Lobey. For their benefit, and for anyone else unfamiliar with the story, an information point has been created.

Apparently, the reason for the statue being erected in Woodlands Road is that the idea for it was conceived in the Halt Bar, across the road from the statue.

Bud Neill's work has enjoyed a renaissance, as, in the late 1990s, some of Lobey's adventures were reprinted in book form, with huge success.

CHAPTER 32

THE 'RESURRECTED' HOUSE
Mackintosh House, Hunterian Museum

Although, at first glance, the building adjoining the Hunterian Museum in Hillhead Street looks like a conventional three-storey house, another look will reveal that its roof is made out of concrete and its front door is in mid-air. The reason for these idiosyncrasies is that the building is a concrete shell hiding the Mackintosh House, a reconstruction of the hall, dining room, studio/drawing room and principal bedroom of 78 Southpark Avenue, the Glasgow home of Charles Rennie Mackintosh and his artist wife, Margaret Macdonald, from 1906 to 1914. (Although the Mackintoshes are always said to have lived at 78 Southpark Avenue, it never was their address. It was actually 6 Florentine Terrace, or 78 Ann Street, as the street was then called. It was not until 1930 that Ann Street became Southpark Avenue, by which time Rennie Mackintosh was dead.)

As the Mackintosh House is sealed into the Hunterian, the only way to view it is to approach from the rear, through the lobby of the gallery.

The Mackintosh house, incorporating the original fenestration and front door

Mackintosh bought 78 Southpark Avenue, a typical mid-19th-century Glasgow terrace house, for £925. It had four floors, four public rooms, five bedrooms, a kitchen, two bathrooms and a garden at the front and back. As well as remodelling the house's proportions and natural lighting, Mackintosh modified the Victorian features by replacing doors, fireplaces, cornices and light fittings. He then furnished it throughout in his own distinctive style. Colour schemes were white, black and muted tones of brown and grey, enhanced by sparing touches of colour in the detailing of furniture and fitments and by the inclusion of the couple's watercolours and decorative panels. (When the Mackintoshes moved out of their previous home, a flat at 120 Mains Street, now Blythswood Street, they dismantled as much of it as they could and reinstalled it at 78 Southpark Avenue.)

A friend of the Mackintoshes, Mary Newberry Sturrock, who visited the house often, said, 'The drawing room was always very simple, giving an impression of withdrawn quiet and repose – nothing lay about accidentally – everything in the room was carefully considered, down to the smallest detail, even grey corduroy cushions, one each side of the fireplace for their grey Persian cats.'

In 1914, the Mackintoshes moved south. His brief time as one of the most influential architects of modern times was over, and he left Glasgow feeling it had abandoned him. The house and most of its contents were bought by William Davidson, for whom Mackintosh had designed Windyhill (1899), a house in Renfrewshire. Following Davidson's death in 1945, the University of Glasgow purchased the property. Concurrently, Davidson's sons, Hamish and Cameron, presented the bulk of the original furniture to the University of Glasgow in memory of their father.

Despite strong protest, the house was demolished in 1963, allegedly because of the threat of subsidence and the university's plans for development nearby. Before demolition, however, a measured survey and photographic record were undertaken, and all fittings, including fireplaces, doors and windows, were carefully removed to enable a future reconstruction of the principal interiors within the then planned Hunterian Museum. (The interiors were those where Mackintosh's main structural alterations had been made and the rooms for which the university owned almost the complete suites of furniture.)

While the architects, Whitfield Partners, conceived the Mackintosh

House as an integral part of the museum, they were painstaking in ensuring that the sequence of rooms reflected the original. They were not constructed as a series of three-sided displays but were rebuilt on three floors, with the original south and east orientation replicating the light that Mackintosh considered an essential part of his interior designs. In this way the atmospheric character of Mackintosh's carefully coordinated interior was recreated. (As the Mackintosh House was only about 100 yards away from 78 Southpark Avenue, the views were virtually the same.) Externally, the 19th-century grey sandstone façade and roof were not recreated. Instead, the shell of the house, like the rest of the museum, was constructed of poured concrete, with the vital details – the fenestration and front door – set off against a harled finish, often favoured by Mackintosh.

Completed in 1981, the reconstructed interiors allow visitors to experience the extraordinary surroundings that the remarkable Mackintoshes created for themselves. They have been furnished with the couple's own furniture and decorated as closely as possible to the original.

As already mentioned, the house is entered via the museum and visitors first come to the Information Room, occupying the floor area of a ground-floor rear room that Mackintosh partitioned in 1906 to form a servant's bedroom and cloakroom. The double doors incorporate panels from the Ingram Street Tea Rooms, acquired in 1971 when the interiors were dismantled by Glasgow Corporation.

Above. Dining room containing the first of Mackintosh's high-back chair designs

Left. The hall with its dark stained wood, leaded-glass pendant light fittings and mirror by Margaret Macdonald, Frances Macdonald and Herbert MacNair

Mackintosh disguised the high narrow hall by replacing the cornice with a simple cove, painted white to blend with the ceiling, and adding dark panelling and wall strapping to lower the eyeline. To provide more light he replaced the narrow upright window with a larger horizontal one. A beaten-lead mirror 'vanity', designed by Margaret and Frances Macdonald and James Herbert in 1896, was placed opposite the window to create an illusion of width. Mackintosh also removed the outer storm doors and replaced them with a single door with a fixed light above.

The hall's colour scheme is simple – white walls and dark woodwork, enriched by the purple glass set in the front door and the pink and silver of the light fittings. (Designed in 1901, the unique pendant light fittings were exhibited in 'The Rose Boudoir', a room setting created by Mackintosh and his wife for the Turin International Exhibition of Modern Decorative Art in 1902. Those on the window wall and the landing are original; the other six are modern replicas.)

The dining room faced east and overlooked the front garden. Mackintosh made few alterations here: the moulded cornice was removed, a picture rail applied and taller doors fitted, their height, and that of the picture rail, being dictated by that of the new front door. The Mains Street dining-room fireplace was installed, with additional shelving at either side to infill the wider chimney breast.

Despite a white frieze and ceiling, the dining room is sombre, with its brown stencilled walls and dark-stained oak furniture. As only two lengths of the wallpaper survive, firm evidence of the original scheme was not available. However, as analysis revealed silver-and-green paint beneath many areas of maroon overpaint, all three colours were emphasised in the new scheme.

Most of the furniture dates from the late 1890s to 1900, the most innovative being the chairs, the first of Mackintosh's trademark 'high-back' designs developed for the Luncheon Room in the Argyle Street Tea Rooms (1897). The table was also based on the design for the Luncheon Room. Of the other furniture, in 1972 Hamish Davidson bequeathed the serving table and the stained-pine sideboard with brass fittings, the earliest piece in the house and possibly the first item designed by Mackintosh for his own use. It was initially, painted white, and he used it at 27 Regent Park Square, his bachelor flat in Glasgow, as a bookcase and drawings cabinet, and then he had it stripped and stained for inclusion in the Mains Street dining room.

Mackintosh achieved the breathtaking lightness of the studio/drawing room by knocking the front drawing room and rear bedroom together, creating an L-shaped space lit from the south, east and west. He also increased the amount of south light by replacing the narrow window at the south-east corner with a larger one. Many Victorian features – fireplaces, doors, light fittings, cornices – were removed or replaced, and a screening wall was constructed above picture-rail level to mask the vertical proportions of the two east windows. The quality of light flooding into the remodelled room was maximised by an all-white décor, any harshness from the sun's rays being softened by muslin curtains.

Although all the furniture in the room is extraordinary, the *pièce de résistance* is the white-painted oak bookcase with leaded glass in a stylised plant design. This amazing piece of furniture, one of the most elegant designs in glass that Macintosh produced, slots into the wall beside the large door with coloured glass set into it that Mackintosh introduced into the room. The bookcase is apparently a variant of the one Mackintosh designed for his brother-in-law, Charles Macdonald, but is more adventurous than the straightforward stem-and-leaf pattern of that piece.

Second to the bookcase is a white-painted oak desk with silvered copper panels showing stylised female figures and rose motifs, which, although unsigned, are believed to be by Margaret Macdonald. The desk is an ingenious design, with deep side cupboards and various internal subdivisions.

The pristine white studio/drawing room with painted oak bookcase and ebonised writing cabinet. The chair was designed to accompany the writing cabinet

There are various tables and chairs in the room designed in Mackintosh's individual style and a wonderful writing cabinet of ebonised mahogany and sycamore with pear-tree, mother-of-pearl, ivory and glass inlays. It also has a metal panel with leaded glass and silver-dipped metal fittings.

While the room is beautiful to look at, it is so minimalist and flawless that there is no room for the everyday things in life. Even a teacup lying on a table would mar its perfection and for a newspaper to be left on a chair would be a crime.

Few alterations were made to the stairwell, except that a new south-facing window was installed and the west stairwell was panelled with dark-stained wood, above which was a plaster panel by Mackintosh based on the design for the Willow Tea Room. The striped stairway led to an attic studio/bedroom, not reconstructed.

As in the studio/drawing room, two rooms were knocked together to create the L-shaped main bedroom, large enough to hold the couple's white-painted oak bedroom furniture with sculptural detailing inspired by plant and bird forms. Mackintosh created a white room setting enlivened by the stencilled fabrics and the glass and painted insets in the furniture, all designed in 1900. The Mains Street bedroom fireplace was installed. (The Mackintoshes must have settled into 78 Southpark Avenue quickly, as so much of it was identical to their former home.)

Above. The main bedroom, again a pristine white room created out of two rooms to accommodate the Mackintosh's white-painted oak suite. The bed was the first four-poster Mackintosh designed.

Right. Guest bedroom furniture at 78 Derngate, 1919. (All photographs copyright Hunterian Art Gallery and Museum, University of Glasgow, Mackintosh Collection)

The principal pieces of furniture in the room are a massive canopied bed (the first four-poster that Mackintosh designed, looking rather like a cubicle), a wardrobe constructed in three sections and an incredible cheval mirror with glass insets and silvered brass handles, which was exhibited in Vienna at the Secessionist exhibition. Above the fireplace is a metal panel by Margaret Macdonald. The bedroom is as unreal as the drawing room. It would be sacrilege to sleep in such a room. Beautiful, but clinical.

Incorporated in the reconstructed 78 Southpark Street is the Mackintosh Gallery, providing a display area for changing selections from the university's extensive collection of Mackintosh's drawings and designs.

On permanent display is a reconstructed room setting with furniture from the guest bedroom at 78 Derngate, Northampton. Mackintosh designed it in 1919 and created a stunningly original interior by introduced a dazzling scheme of black, white and ultramarine, in which linear and geometric motifs predominate. The simple furniture relies for effect on contrasting grains and on striking blue-and-black edging. The black-and-white stripe of the bedspreads is picked up on the wall and ceiling by a patterned paper that suggests a canopy linking the two beds. While the white bedroom of Southpark Avenue is beautiful but clinical, this bedroom is beautiful but warm.

It is no wonder that Mackintosh's interior design was looked upon as extremist. It was totally unlike the typical style of his time. There were no antimacassars, gilded picture frames, whatnots, potted palms or bric-à-brac. Instead, he favoured white décor, the minimum of furniture and plain unlined muslin curtains to let the sunlight filter in. Here and there, a few carefully chosen objects were scattered round the rooms, which, to most people, were shockingly bare.

Mackintosh's rooms cannot be confused with those of his many imitators. They are instantly recognisable as his by their purity, freshness and, above all, astounding originality. (Although Mackintosh designed hundreds of pieces of furniture, he never repeated himself.) It can be said that Mackintosh's great strength as a decorator was that his rooms were conceived as a whole – he designed every piece in them.

Although the 'resurrected' Mackintosh House attracts thousands of visitors from all corners of the world, many Glaswegians have never set foot inside it. A case of not appreciating what is on your own doorstep.

CHAPTER 33

THE TUNNEL BENEATH THE CLYDE

Harbour Tunnel, Finnieston to Govan

The two domed rotundas on each bank of the Clyde were not built just as landmarks; they hid the entrances to the Harbour Tunnel, running south from Tunnel Street in Finnieston under the river to Mavisbank Quay in Govan.

Until the Harbour Tunnel was built, the Jamaica Bridge (or Glasgow Bridge) was the farthest downstream crossing of the Clyde, apart from the ferries. Attempts had been made to bridge the river farther downstream but they were always opposed on the grounds that river traffic would be obstructed.

The Glasgow Harbour Tunnel Co. began excavating in 1890 and opened for traffic on 15 July 1895. A rotunda on each bank of the river marked the ends of the Harbour Tunnel and, directly below them, vertical shafts 80 feet in diameter gave access to three tunnels – two between 16 and 18 feet in

Inside the passenger tunnel, which also held giant water pipes

diameter for vehicular traffic (then horse-drawn vehicles) and one for pedestrians, nine feet in diameter. The pedestrian tunnel shared its brick-glazed passage with a water main.

Supplied by the Otis Company of New York, six hydraulically powered vehicle lift cages in the rotundas took the wheeled traffic down to the tunnels. Each lift operated independently, and elaborate open winding gear filled the upper area of the rotundas. A long flight of dimly lit steps provided direct access to the pedestrian tunnel, independent of the vehicle tunnels. Charges were 3d for horsedrawn vehicles, 1d for a man with a wheelbarrow and 1/2d for pedestrians or a flock of sheep.

Construction achievements were never matched by commercial success. The Harbour Tunnel was a financial disaster and the tunnels were closed in 1907, remaining so until 1913 when the Corporation leased them and reopened them as a free service. Four years later the pedestrian tunnel was closed, and pedestrians had to use the vehicle tunnels and the lifts that descended among a bewildering medley of wheels and cables through which could be seen the mouth of the disused pedestrian tunnel. In 1926, the city bought the network for £100,000, against an initial construction cost 30 years earlier of £287,000.

Traffic kept to the left in the tunnels so that it was always going in the

The north rotunda which, in the 1990s became a restaurant and casino. The giant Finnieston crane towers above the rotunda.

one direction in each tunnel. Although the tunnels were lit by electricity, it could be quite frightening going through them, as the clattering hooves of the horses echoed loudly in the confined space. The fact that water oozed through the iron sides of the great pipe did not help, for, since the Harbour Tunnel opened, it had never been possible to make it watertight. It was also known for stalactites to hang from the roof like white daggers. Understandably, except perhaps on wet days, the tunnel was never as popular as on the nearby ferry.

Vehicular traffic through the tunnels was stopped in 1943, and the aged lift machinery was removed for scrap. Pedestrian access was reinstated in 1947. When in use, the pedestrian tunnel had to be manned around the clock and, with the maintenance needs, the system required a full-time staff of 20 men. As the general area became run-down, however, the tunnel's use declined from a mid-1950s' figure of 1,500 pedestrians daily to around 200 when it closed on 4 April 1980. A survey showed that only 211 people had used the route between 6.00 am and 10.00 pm on a weekday in January 1980.

After that, the tunnels were forgotten about until the issue of re-opening them was raised during the run-up to the Garden Festival, when it was pointed out that they provided a ready-made route to the Festival and were a wasted asset. When it was decided instead to build Bell's Bridge across the river, however, the fate of the tunnels was sealed and, in 1986, the vehicle shafts were closed and the access shafts filled in. The pedestrian link was kept open for access to the water mains.

The Garden Festival in 1988 did bring some new life to the rotundas. The north building was given a facelift and the south one prospered as a cafeteria run by the famous ice-cream maker, Nardini. The cafeteria, a replica, down to the last detail, of Nardini's legendary seafront Continental Café in Largs, featured all-Scottish fresh produce. In 1990, as part of the Glasgow City of Culture celebrations the south rotunda was briefly transformed into a Dome of Discovery, a hands-on science exhibition. In the 1990s, the north rotunda became a restaurant and casino.

During the late 1920s and 1930s, there was a long-running campaign to build a bridge at Finnieston, which was unsuccessful. By 2000, history had repeated itself, as there was controversy about a proposed bridge at Finnieston to connect with the rotunda on Govan Road. Maybe the Harbour Tunnel should be re-opened.

CHAPTER 34

NEGLECTED GRANDEUR

Laurieston House, Carlton Place

No one would guess the impressive exterior of Laurieston House in Carlton Place conceals the decaying interior of what is possibly Britain's finest Georgian house. The building was built in 1806 by wealthy Glasgow merchant James Laurie, who decided to create a suburb of middle- to high-class dwellings, with Carlton Place as its frontage and his own extraordinary home at the heart of it.

Laurie's suburb, Glasgow's first planned development south of the river, failed for several reasons. There was tight competition from other developments within the city and, as Glasgow was beginning to explode in size with the Industrial Revolution, demand in the area was for low-cost housing and industrial premises rather than good-quality accommodation.

Laurie, a ruthless businessman who traded from America to Europe, was one of the breed of middle-class merchants, who, having made their fortunes, wanted to show that the merchant class could match, or outmatch, the landed gentry. This he did by making Laurieston House the finest home in the city.

As an indication of how important the fine old mansion was in its day, it was chosen to accommodate George IV when he was expected to visit

The impressive exterior of Laurieston House in Carlton Place

Glasgow on his trip to Scotland in 1822. Unfortunately, the Glasgow part of the king's itinerary was not carried out, so the house does not have that memory to add to its history. What it can boast is that it had no fewer than four water closets, one on each floor, the water for which was pumped up from the basement. (Early closets were about five feet square with no ventilation, and it was not until the end of the 19th century that the rooms were lighted and ventilated to the outside by means of a window in a back or front wall.)

Luckily, there are detailed records of Laurieston, which was built by architect Peter Nicolson. Actually, it was lucky for historians, not for Laurie, as the records are available only because he went bankrupt in 1817, the sequestration document containing a full inventory of the house. Every stick of furniture, every book, every painting, every glass and even the teaspoons were carefully noted and valued. (Laurie continued to live in the house until his death in 1853, by which time he had recouped his wealth.)

Among the records is a copy of Laurie's will, which shows that, after he died, the estate was broken up among his family. His family tree is also available and reveals that he and his wife, Helen, had 14 children, only five of whom, all girls, survived to adulthood. As Laurie had no son to carry on the family name, he insisted that his daughters used it in a hyphenated form when they married.

Laurieston House is a Grade A-listed building for various reasons – its place within the whole terrace, also listed; its unusual design (four floors at the back and three at the front); and the fact that it is really two neighbouring houses run together to make one. The main reason, however, is the plasterwork, which is sumptuous for the time, as Georgian interiors tended to be austere. (Charlotte Square in Edinburgh and Royal Terrace in Bath are quite plain.)

Above. Details of the stunning plasterwork in the porch

Left. The dining room of Laurieston House around 1850, showing the sideboard built into a recess

The Strathclyde Building Preservation Trust is bringing the property to life again after decades of neglect. Immediately inside the two front doors, it becomes obvious why the house is so special, as the heavily ornamented plasterwork in the porch is stunning. It's the work of Francisco Bernasconi, brought to Britain by George III to decorate Windsor Castle.

When the Trust acquired the neglected building, last occupied by Strathclyde Regional Social Work Department, all the beams had rotted and water was running down the walls. Before any restoration work to return the interior to its former glory could begin, the building had to be made structurally secure and watertight. Among other things, a new main roof was put on and the stonework on the façade, particularly at the top of the pediment, repaired. The foundations, which had pretty much disappeared, were stabilised by pumping concrete into them. In fact, some of the foundations are still on show, as the dining room has an alarming hole in the floor, taking up half the room.

Laid out in the dining room are plans showing the layout of the pair of houses making up Laurieston. The two houses are a mirror image of each other, except that the centre line is slightly offset, making the west house slightly larger. Also displayed is a blown-up copy of a photograph of the dining room, taken around 1850, which shows, among the furniture, a curved sideboard with a statuette sitting at each end of it. Apparently, the sideboard was built into a recess so that none of the floor space would be lost and, as both it and the statuettes were included in the bankruptcy inventory, somehow Laurie must have done a deal to keep the house and the contents.

Although the photograph shows the edge of a ceiling rose that no longer exists, the rest of the magnificent plasterwork remains, as does the circular wax plaque showing Hector and Andromache, and Aeneas carrying Anchises. As much of the plaster ornamentation has a classical theme, it is believed that Bernasconi's work, along with that of other craftsmen, was influenced by the excavations at Pompeii and Herculaneum at the time.

The elegant main staircase, lit by an oval cupola supported on Corinthian pillars filled in with panels containing classic figures of Castor and Pollux and the three Graces, leads to the library, a curious room with more doors than walls. Laurie must have been obsessed with symmetry, for, in this room as well as others, he had dummy doors installed to balance the real doors at corresponding parts in the room's walls. One door opens into a large cupboard, which appears to have been used as a safe for it has a heavy steel door half an inch thick. Even the bookcases have doors and, following the space-saving ideas seen elsewhere in the house, are set into the wall. Classical Greek and Roman scenes, garlands and medallions decorate what wall space there is. The panel over where the mantelpiece was tells the story of 'The Temptations of Hercules'.

A full-size statue of ther Roman goddess Minerva stands in a niche on the drawing-room landing. Facing the landing is an archway decorated with classical figures, above which is a round hole in the wall, surrounded by graceful plaster ornamentation. The hole housed a large clock, which was wound and set by means of an ingenious arrangement in a little cupboard that lies behind it through the wall on the inside concealed stair that leads to the bedrooms. The clock has been removed for safety during the restoration work.

The large drawing room, with three windows facing the river, has more dummy doors and a ceiling and cornice decorated with graceful plasterwork. This room holds another of the house's curiosities – a floor hung on chains or rods in such a way as to make the tension adjustable. Whether it is true or not, there is a story that when balls were held in the room, depending on the style of dance, a slow one like a waltz or a fast one like a polka, the tension was adjusted to the bounce level of the floor.

Connecting with the drawing room is the ante-drawing or tea room, once the domain of the ladies of the house. It's elliptical in form and, in two niches made in the walls, are life-size figures of the Roman goddesses Ceres and Flora. Sadly, by the early 1950s, the ceiling was in such a dangerous condition that it had to be taken down, destroying the rich ornamentation in the process. This room contains one of the most curious arrangements in a house full of curiosities – a curved door opening into a small triangular space, the other two sides of which consist of matching curved doors. One door conceals a large cupboard, the other leads to the drawing-room landing, the idea being that servants could tend to the ladies' needs without having to disturb the men by going through the drawing room.

As only the principal rooms were accessed by the staircase, it goes no farther than the drawing room. Everywhere else was accessed from a secondary staircase to the rear, an arrangement that meant the public areas of the house and the private areas could be completely separate.

It is surprising that what was once the master bedroom is devoid of the plasterwork so abundant in the public rooms. It is very plain, which might be because it was more in keeping with the period of the house or, more likely, that because the bedrooms were not on show, there was no need to waste money on ornamenting them.

Visible in the bedroom through the holes in the floor and walls is the strange system of rods and chains that help to support one of the bedroom walls and the tension in the drawing-room floor.

From the bedroom, there's a bird's-eye view of the house's second domed cupola and the fine plasterwork around it. Surrounding the landing is a wrought-iron balcony, where, it is said, all the young ladies would congregate whenever James Laurie was having a party so that they could eye up the men coming up the main staircase into the drawing room and choose which ones they fancied as dancing partners.

Although there are many curiosities in Laurieston, the most curious of all must be that it is really two houses in one, each a mirror image of the other, except, as already mentioned, that the centre line is slightly offset, making the west house slightly larger. Another difference is that, although the interior ornamentation is almost identical, it was slightly less lavish in the smaller house.

It has been suggested that one side of the house was intended for Laurie's brother but, as the Lauries had such a large family, they would have needed both houses to fit everyone in, as there were only six bedrooms between the two houses. Maybe the adults used one side of the house and the children the other.

Minerva standing guard outside the drawing room

To date, it has cost around £1.6 million just to make the building structurally secure and watertight, and the same amount is needed to finish the job, which will take a few more years. Fortunately, however, most of the sumptuous plasterwork has survived more or less intact.

John King who, before he retired, was Secretary of the Strathclyde Building Preservation Trust, said that when he first came to Glasgow he could not believe that the city had such a magnificent house right in the centre. He had travelled through the UK, Europe and North America and had never come across anything like it. James Laurie would have agreed with him.